MANAGING THE MULTI-GENERATIONAL WORKFORCE

Managing the Multi-Generational Workforce

From the GI Generation to the Millennials

Robert G. DelCampo,
Lauren A. Haggerty,
Meredith Jane Haney
and
Lauren Ashley Knippel

GOWER

Gower Applied Business Research
Our programme provides leaders, practitioners, scholars and researchers with thought provoking, cutting edge books that combine conceptual insights, interdisciplinary rigour and practical relevance in key areas of business and management.

Published by
Gower Publishing Limited
Wey Court East
Union Road
Farnham
Surrey GU9 7PT
England

Gower Publishing Company
Suite 420
101 Cherry Street
Burlington, VT 05401-4405
USA

www.gowerpublishing.com

British Library Cataloguing in Publication Data
Managing the multi-generational workforce : from the GI
  generation to the millennials.
  1. Personnel management. 2. Diversity in the workplace. 3. Intergenerational relations.
  I. DelCampo, Robert G.
  658.3'0084-dc22

ISBN: 978-1-4094-0388-3 (pbk); 978-1-4094-0389-0 (ebk)

Library of Congress Cataloging-in-Publication Data
Managing the multi-generational workforce : from the GI generation to the millennials
/ by Robert G. DelCampo ... [et al.].
    p. cm.
  Includes bibliographical references and index.
  ISBN 978-1-4094-0388-3 (pbk.) -- ISBN 978-1-4094-0389-0 (ebook)
  1. Diversity in the workplace--Management. 2. Conflict of generations.
  3. Intergenerational relations. 4. Personnel management. I. DelCampo, Robert G.
  HF5549.5.M5M364 2010
  658.3--dc22

2010015704

MIX
Paper from
responsible sources
FSC® C013056
www.fsc.org

Printed and bound in Great Britain by
TJ International Ltd, Padstow, Cornwall.

Contents

v

List of Tables

About the Authors

ROBERT G. DELCAMPO, PH.D

Dr. Robert G. (Rob) DelCampo is an Associate Professor in the Department of Organization Studies at the University of New Mexico, holding the Rutledge Endowed Professorship in Management. His teaching interests lie in Organizational Behavior and Human Resource Management, while his research interest focus on the underrepresented members of the workforce (Hispanics in particular), work-family conflict, turnover and psychological contracts.

He currently serves as Editor-in-Chief of *Administrative Sciences* and Associate Editor of *The Business Journal of Hispanic Research* and was recently named to New Mexico Business Weekly's "40 Under 40" top young professional list and one of Albuquerque *The Magazine*'s "15 People Who Will Change Albuquerque". Rob has published or presented over 75 papers and is the author of 5 books. He has consulted for over 25 Fortune 500 companies including Ford, Home Depot, Dell and Intel. Rob earned a Ph.D. from the W. P. Carey School of Business at Arizona State University in Tempe, AZ in 2004, and holds MBA and undergraduate degrees from the University of New Mexico in Albuquerque.

LAUREN HAGGERTY

Lauren attended the University of New Mexico earning degrees in Accounting (BBA) and Organizational Behavior/Human Resources (MBA). Currently, she works in Student Affairs at the University of New Mexico where she deals with Millennials on a day-to-day basis.

MEREDITH JANE HANEY

Born and raised in Albuquerque, NM, Meredith attended the University of New Mexico where she attained a Bachelor's in Business Administration with a focus in Accounting in 2007. She earned her MBA concentrating in Management Information Systems, Information Assurance, and Organizational Behavior/Human Resources from the Anderson Schools of Management at the University of New Mexico in 2009.

LAUREN ASHLEY KNIPPEL

Born in 1985 and raised in Albuquerque, NM, Lauren graduated with her Bachelor's in Business Administration in 2007 with a focus in Human Resources and Organizational Leadership from the Anderson Schools of Management at the University of New Mexico. She attained her MBA concentrating in Strategic Planning in 2009.

Foreword

In case you hadn't heard, the multi-generational workplace is now a reality. *Managing the Multi-Generational Workforce: From the G. I. Generation to the Millennials* provides an excellent analysis of the issues generated by a multi-generational workforce and gives keen insight into how to garner the unique voice of our newest generation, the Millennials, in order to capitalize on the most critical resource of the workplace—the employees. If you wonder if Millennials are really all they are cracked up to be, you have to look no further than this book to understand the potential that Millennials offer organizations.

The authors, Robert G. DelCampo, Lauren A. Haggerty, Meredith Jane Haney, and Lauren Ashley Knippel, a team of experts in the field of human resources management, have written a clear, highly readable volume focused on managing differences across generations by embracing those differences for maximum organizational effectiveness. In his short career, Rob DelCampo has produced more meaningful contributions to the profession than academics twice his age. He is passionate about his research and has expanded the theory and practice of diversity and inclusiveness through his work. Rob and his co-authors deserve high accolades for conceiving and writing this book that explains employee differences through a backdrop of generations. The time-line approach to defining workers by their place in history is an easy one to grasp and profoundly unique in the insights it brings.

In my 20-plus years as a university management professor specializing in human resources, I have taught members of each of the generations profiled in this book. Human resources management focuses on using organizational resources efficiently and effectively. This book will show employers how to do just that—how to understand the multi-generations they have working for them, from the G.I. Generation to the Millennials, how to best manage them, and how to embrace their unique talents, skills, and abilities to enhance the organization now and in the future. This book introduces a perspective of managing the workplace by embracing diversity across generations and offers a unique outlook that will help managers and researchers alike as they strive to understand the similarities and differences of workers to better utilize all of their strengths to create the organization of the twenty-first century.

Strategically managing the multi-generational workforce to create a strong organization poised to meet the uncertainties of a turbulent market economy is a formidable challenge, now more than ever. That is why this book is so important. The book has something to offer readers of all generations. While other books have dealt with the struggles presented by multi-generations at work, this text brings the Millennials into the workplace and presents them to us as all grown up and ready to take on the world. In this book, Rob DelCampo and his co-authors illustrate that Millennials in the workforce are here to stay. They are a growing presence and a group that will have a major impact on organizations now and in the years to come.

Rob and his team are right—the Millennial generation is unique. The authors critically and comprehensively examine our newest generation of workers. They demonstrate that the Millennials are workers who are poised to lead organizations into the future—but only if employers understand what these workers want, what they expect from the organization, and what they are willing to give in return. Especially useful in the book is the discussion of the complexity of designing an organizational culture and structure to meet the needs of the multi-generational workforce, and of the need for that culture to reflect the expectations of the Millennials in order to effectively attract and retain the talent and potential these workers will offer employers.

Being the product of a generation prior to the Millennials (I won't say which for fear of further aging myself) I can say that I have often not understood the behaviors of the Millennials I encounter and the choices I have seen them make about their lives. I know they baffle employers with their desires for challenging but meaningful jobs, with their demand for leisure time away from work, and with their "interesting" choices in wardrobe and body art! But this book will clearly show us what positive assets the Millennials are if we embrace their strengths and truly believe they have something to say to us. Rob's book shows us exactly what we are missing if we fail to take advantage of the skills and abilities the Millennials present.

Rob and his team show us the reasons why Millennials are exceptional and how they really could be our greatest generation yet. The Millennials have expertise and knowledge that we do not—for example, they understand technology and use it like another appendage. They are not afraid of new ideas. They have grown up with diversity in their classrooms and their activities, and they welcome it now. They are quick to laugh and quick to critique, not automatically accepting the status quo as the only way to get things done. Yes, they demand a lot, but look what they have accomplished in their short lives.

The multi-generational workplace can mean many changes for members of earlier generations who are perfectly content with doing things the way they always have. Change is hard, but change can be good—if we give it a chance. I have an exercise I do with my students to introduce the notion of change. First, I make them get up and move two seats down and one seat over from their "normal" pre-chosen seat. I never assign seats—they choose their own, and everyone respects the choices their classmates make. Disrupting their routine is an instant way to introduce the concept of change. Then I tell them the story about the roast. Here's how it goes: There was once a woman preparing a roast for Sunday dinner. As she started, she cut off the end of the roast before she put it in the pot. Her husband asked why she did that. She said she wasn't sure, but that was the way her mother had always made her roast. So she called her mother to find out why. "Mom," she said, "why do you always cut the end of the roast off before you put it in the pot?" "Because that's the way your grandmother always did it and I learned from her. Why don't you call her and ask her." So the woman called her grandmother and said, "Grandma, why do you always cut the end of the roast off before you put it in the pot?" "Because," her grandmother said, "the pot is small and that is the only way the roast will fit". So, three generations of cooks had prepared the roast the same way, but two had no idea why. Sometimes there can initially be a good reason for a certain business practice, but that practice gets passed on for reasons that no longer exist.

The Millennials in our workplaces are challenging the established norms of business practice. Why work in an office when they can work at home? Why should they respect someone just because of their age or position? Millennials dare those members of earlier generations to rethink the way business is done. They are more open to change and new ideas and will confront us when they think we are wrong. In my classroom teaching, my Millennial students will often ask why they have to learn something. The challenge is to prove what we do is relevant to them and then they will embrace it.

I came away from reading this wonderful, groundbreaking book with a new appreciation of Millennials and a new understanding of what they can bring to the workplace. Whether you are an employer or not, this is a must read because it gives us a comprehensive picture of Millennials and defines their important place in the multi-generational workplace we all face on a daily basis. Look around you—look at your co-workers right now—and you will see that whether we like it or not, we are part of a multi-generational workforce that must embrace its newest members. It is natural for each generation to view the workplace from its own perspective. Just as two people can look at the same picture and see two different things, this books helps us see the workplace from the Millennials' perspective. It shows us why we may have misjudged them if we apply our values and experiences to them and expect them to be the kind of employees we are. They are not. They may be better.

The book is a must read for academics, business people, managers, and leaders alike. It describes the challenges of dealing with multi-generations in the workforce while offering sound rationale for those differences and strategic solutions for managing those generations for success. I wholeheartedly agree with Rob's conclusions that communication, valuing differences as strengths instead of seeing them as weaknesses, and creating a culture of cooperation in the spirit of working together to meet organizational goals are all essential to building a successful workplace in the twenty-first century.

The Millennials are poised to become our greatest generation yet. They work together. They embrace groups and collaborate. They are forward-thinking, positive, and achieve what they set their sights on. As the authors aptly attest, the Millennials are the heroes of the workplace today. Thanks to Rob DelCampo and his co-authors, we now understand what Millennials expect from the workplace, what they want, how they relate to other generations, how to attract and retain them, and how to manage them within the context of the multi-generational workforce. It is knowledge that is essential for organizations if they expect to survive and thrive now and in the future.

Teresa L. Smith, Ph.D
Julian T. Buxton Professor of Business Administration
University of South Carolina, U.S.A.

Introduction

For the first time in the history of the United States, five generations are alive simultaneously. This includes the GI Generation (1925–1945), Traditionalists (1925–1945), Baby Boomers (1946–1964), Generation X (1965–1980), and Millennials (1981–2000s) (Underwood 2007). While generational gaps have always existed at work, the vast increase in life expectancies during this century has resulted in the latter four generations working side by side (Lancaster & Stillman 2002). This phenomenon has been perpetuated by increased life expectancy and a delay in retirement.

Academic research in management has noted that generations are an ideal taxonomy for grouping individuals as this creates a context for common attitudes and behaviors at work (Dencker, Joshi & Martocchio 2007, 2008) while sociologists note that generational groups create unique identities and collective sets of memories (Griffin 2004, Schuman & Scott 1989, 2004). Through any of these lenses, generations can be viewed as an approximation of the collective set of attitudes, behaviors, ideals, memories, and life experiences that will certainly affect work-life. While the exact definition of a "generation" has been of some debate (see Chapter 1), the most common and accepted definition is a concept bound to the realm of kinship and descent or a cohort of individuals of similar exposures and experiences (Kertzer 1983).

In the next few years, the increased retirement of Baby Boomers will undoubtedly lead to a shortage of workers. It is estimated that in 2010, 64 million Baby Boomers, who make up 40 percent of the workforce, will be poised for retirement ("Gen Yers Changing" 2007). A combination of retiring Baby Boomers and Traditionalists leads to the prediction that there will be a lack of individuals in place for upper management positions (Lancaster & Stillman 2002). This prediction is based upon the fact that Generation X consists of slightly more than half the total number of Baby Boomers (Lancaster & Stillman 2002). In addition to Baby Boomers retiring, members of Generation X are also choosing to leave the workforce in favor of spending time with family or reducing long work hours (Trunk 2007). This leads to the census data prediction that as each new hire enters the workforce, two employees will be leaving (Gerdes 2006). While the number of employees decreases, it is expected that the demand for them will increase. Over the next 25 years, predictions show that "demand for bright, talented 35 to 45-year-olds will increase by 25 percent, while supply will decrease by 15 percent" (Lancaster & Stillman 2002: 6). Clearly, the business world will have to rely on the Millennial generation to fill in the void left behind by retiring Traditionalists and Baby Boomers.

Although each generation is important, understanding the characteristics, behaviors, and expectations of the Millennial generation is the key to future success. As the other generations have been present in the workforce for a longer period of time, managers have already established a knowledge base and managerial techniques for these cohorts. In order to provide managers with the most pertinent information concerning the workforce today and that of the future, this book will dedicate significant attention to Millennials but will also focus on the issues associated with clashing values, beliefs, and attitudes inherent in a multi-generational workforce.

This text is unique in that it is written by Millennials (and one Gen X-er) for this very same audience. While many popular press articles and texts discuss the "problems" with Millennials we approach them as "different" not "bad". Millennials have certain unique characteristics that not only make them distinctly different but also characteristics that make them essential to business success as we move further into the twenty-first century. We hope that this overview of the multi-generational workforce is a quick and stimulating read that enhances the readers' thirst for further knowledge on this topic. While there is scant research surrounding generations at work, we tie together this academic research, anecdotal evidence, and popular press reports to give an overview of the issues we face in today's multi-generational workforce.

(1) Overview of the Generations

WHAT IS A GENERATION?

Generations are defined as "an 'age cohort' that shares unique formative years' experiences and teachings (roughly the first 20 to 23 years of their lives) and thus develop unique core values and attitudes that are different from other generations" (Underwood 2007: 43). Life experiences directly influence members of each generation during critical development stages and have a significant effect on the values and beliefs a person carries with them throughout the course of their life. The common influences that can determine shared characteristics of a generation can include parental guidance, interactions with peers, media, and popular culture (Twenge & Campbell 2008).

A generation's ages or birth years serve as the primary guidelines when defining the characteristics of its members, but the true divisions lie in cultural differences. In addition to the common influences, economic and political events that take place during the critical development stages have a significant effect on the way they work or view employment (Dittmann 2005). Generational characteristics influence lifelong decision making. Choices made about which career to choose, products to buy, and types of lifestyle to lead are largely determined by generational context (Underwood 2007). While not every individual will possess all characteristics of their generation, understanding the context in which each generation was formed provides essential information for understanding how to recruit, train, and retain members of each separate group.

DEFINING THE GENERATIONS AS ARCHETYPES

Throughout American history, four specific types of people have evolved (Howe & Strauss 2007). The *Harvard Business Review* outlined several "archetypes" that are created as a result of the events and challenges the people belonging to them face, how they are raised, and how they were taught to prepare for various situations. When the different generations of people living in the United States are broken down into specific archetypes, it is much easier to predict future trends and to forecast how future generations will be raised, including what generations will be like through young adulthood as established adults and as elders in their societies. The archetypes defined by the *Harvard Business Review* include Prophets, Nomads, Heroes, and Artists (Howe & Strauss 2007).

Prophets are born after a large event, usually a crisis, at a time when society is undergoing a rejuvenation period. The children of this type of generation are often overindulged and tend to be passionate about their moral beliefs during the years in which they grow from adolescents to adults. Based on history, this generation will most likely accept the role of elders in the community who lead younger generations through another major crisis. They tend to focus mainly on creating a vision for the future, maintaining values, and practicing some type of religion or faith (Howe & Strauss 2007). In terms of the generations present in the workforce today, Baby Boomers are categorized as Prophets.

As children of the Prophets, Nomads have very different values than their parents. They have been raised to place great value on liberty, survival, and honor. They are typically under-protected by their parents, or those who raise them, as society is usually in a state of cultural rejuvenation. Because of the state of society during these periods, adult members focus on carrying out their spiritual and socially idealistic agendas, rather than placing all of their attention on their children (Howe & Strauss 2007). While the Prophets were born just after a major event, members of the Nomad archetype become adults during a time of crisis (Howe & Strauss 2007). As a result of this, Nomads tend to demonstrate no-nonsense attitudes and a proactive work ethic in the workplace, especially when leading others (Howe & Strauss 2007). Generation X takes on the characteristics of the Nomads archetype.

The next archetype, Heroes represents individuals born during a time of independence when society has embraced a matter-of-fact outlook. Heroes are characterized as individuals that grew up in overprotective environments. As this group matures, they are said to develop into energetic and motivated people that value team work. In fully matured adulthood, Heroes take on a holier-than-thou attitude with an overload of confidence as a result of their upbringing in an overprotective and excessively praise-oriented environment. Additionally, these groups tend to emerge as leaders later in life. The innate qualities associated with Heroes are community, affluence, and technology (Howe & Strauss 2007). Millennials are the Heroes of the workplace today.

The final archetype, Artists, come into the world during war time or an economic depression. The necessity to simplify life and life within one's means defines the environment in which this group is raised. Like Heroes, Artists grow up in overprotective homes. They materialize as young adults who are sensitive to the effects of the crisis they endured in young development stages. They tend to be indecisive as adults in mid-life and compassionate as elders. The Artists are attributed with pluralism, expertise, and due process (Howe & Strauss 2007). Both the Traditionalist Generation and the newly emerging generation, that has yet to be definitively named, fall into the Artist category.

WHO ARE THE CURRENT GENERATIONS?

Because there are no definitive dates by which to categorize each generation, there are generally accepted ranges that most researchers recognize, give or take a few years in either direction. Although each generation possesses characteristics that are defined by common experiences, some major events can be coined as having a "crossover effect." This means that all generations living at the time the event occurred are affected, and thus may develop similar characteristics in relation to it (Patota, Schwartz, & Schwartz 2007).

THE GI GENERATION (born approximately between 1925 and 1942)

The Silent generation, (sometimes referred to as Traditionalists), experienced the conformity of the 1930s through 1960s and the patriotism from the Second World War that aided a notion of community cooperation. They also witnessed the changes of the 1960s that led to women's movements and passage of the Civil Rights Acts. With births ranging from approximately from 1925 to 1942, this generation values safety, including job security. After witnessing the Great Depression, they found themselves simply happy to be employed (Lancaster & Stillman 2002). Despite the fact that retirement is viewed as an earned privilege for years of hard work, many members of this generation work beyond retirement age (Underwood 2007).

BABY BOOMERS (born approximately between 1946 and 1964)

Next are the Baby Boomers, a dominant generation that in their time defied many records by being the largest population. As a generation that resulted from the significant birth increase at the end of the Second World War, the beginning of this generation is well-defined as 1946, and the end is estimated to be near 1964 (Patota, Schwartz, & Schwartz 2007). Boomers are competitors that dedicated their lives to jobs. For the first time, many parents had dual careers which led to personal struggles and increased divorce rates. This generation has modeled idealism, but often found themselves "time poor" in their rush to achieve it all (Underwood 2007: 42). Their great dedication to careers has led the majority of boomers to claim that they will never retire (Lancaster & Stillman 2002). Still, statistics are proving that statement false as they currently retire at a rate of over 8,000 per day (Lies 2007).

GENERATION X (born approximately between 1965 and 1980)

In the shadow of the Baby Boomers, Generation X challenged their optimistic example with defiance. Gen X, presently ages

28 to 48, is best known for being negative, cynical, and skeptical (Braid 2007). Although they experienced a comfortable childhood, they resented workaholic and divorcing parents while observing governmental corruptions such as Watergate (Underwood 2007). Their self-centered focus has led to being less loyal to employers and desiring quicker achievements (Dittmann 2005). Therefore, they frequently job-hop and prefer creative, entrepreneurial ventures (Underwood 2007).

THE MILLENNIAL GENERATION (born between 1981 and 2000)

They have been called Generation Y, Generation Next, the Net Generation, Echo Boomers, iGeneration, Generation Me, the Next Great Generation, and MySpace Generation, but they may be best known as Millennials. As the newest generation joins the workforce, many managers may ask what makes this group different from the past; however, the generational characteristics that define Millennials cannot be ignored. As the quickest growing segment of the workforce, the Millennials experienced an increased presence from 14 to 21 percent in the years 2001–2005 (Armour 2005). This generation is the "largest demographic bulge since the baby boomers" (Aschoff, 2006: 1). Universum Communications, a global research company, said that corporations seeking information about this generation increased 45 percent over a six-month period in 2006 (Gerdes 2006). The unfounded growth of this generation, combined with the imminent decline of the prominent older generations, has provided Millennials a bright future in the workplace.

Each generation has distinct characteristics defined by birth years and important events endured, as well as diverse strengths and weaknesses. The table below, adapted from

Patota, Schwartz, and Schwartz (2007) demonstrates these unique differences observed by each of the generations in the workforce.

Table 1.1   Synopsis of generations

Generation	Other Names	Year of Birth (approx.)	Values	Work-Related Values	World Events/ Innovations
GI	Traditional Conservatives Silent Mature	1925–1945	Conformism Thrift Maturity	Obedience Loyalty Obligation Security	Great Depression Second World War
Baby Boomers	Boom(er) Me Generation	1946–1964	Idealism Creativity Tolerance Freedom	Workaholism Criticism Innovation	Kennedy Assassinations MLK Assassination Vietnam War Moon Landing 1960s Counterculture Movement
Generation X	Xers 13th Generation	1965–1980	Individualism Skepticism Flexibility	Learning Entrepreneurial Spirit Materialism	Oral Contraceptives "The Pill" Cold War
Generation Y	Millennials Generation Next	1981– 2000s	Moralism Confidence Positivity Environmental Consciousness	Passion Balance Leisure Security	Internet MTV 9/11 Attacks Fall of the Eastern Bloc

(Some table information adapted from Dries, Pepermans, De Kerpel 2008)

GENERATIONAL STRENGTHS AND WEAKNESSES

It is important for managers to be aware of the applicable strengths and weaknesses of each generational group. Having a strong understanding of their strengths and weaknesses is key to obtaining the maximum amount of benefit from each employee. Although some strengths and weaknesses are determined on an individual basis, the generational guidelines provide a solid baseline upon which managers can begin learning about their employees.

Traditionalists are known for their accountability, clear communication, management of resources, organization/ management, service orientation, and ability to work collaboratively with others. In terms of weaknesses, Traditionalists tend to struggle with adaptability, initiative, technology, valuing diversity, delaying rewards, and valuing training (Patota, Schwartz, & Schwartz 2007).

Baby Boomers are attributed with excelling in terms of accountability, adaptability, clear communication, initiative, organization/project management, problem solving, service orientation, and working collaboratively. Conversely, they are also known for several weaknesses including the need for instant gratification, technology, and valuing diversity (Patota, Schwartz, & Schwartz 2007).

Generation X is recognized as a generational cohort that shines in terms of adaptability, initiative, managing resources, problem solving, technology, valuing diversity, and value-training. The areas in which they struggle include failing to speak in layman's terms, organization/project management, service orientation, working collaboratively, and loyalty to the organization (Patota, Schwartz, & Schwartz 2007).

Finally, Millennials are noted as a group that embraces accountability, organization/project management, service organization, technology, valuing diversity, and working collaboratively. Drawbacks of this group include communicating informally with text messages, problem solving, loyalty to the organization or lack thereof, and the reliance on technology as integral to life style (Patota, Schwartz, & Schwartz 2007).

In a diverse workplace, the value of each generational cohort provides unique value based on its specific traits and characteristics, expectations, values, strengths, and weaknesses. Managers should strive to develop an appreciation for the benefits each generation has to offer. The following chapters provide more information about, and analysis of, the pertinent aspects of effective management for each generation.

② Millennials

Millennials (sometimes called Generation Y) have been a part of the corporate world for a relatively short period of time in comparison to the other three generations in the workforce. Because this large group of young people have entered the current workforce in mass numbers and will undoubtedly continue to grow over the next few years, managers must pay special attention to the different expectations, values, needs, and desires of this generation. In order to fully understand the complexity of Millennials as working professionals, a breadth of knowledge must first be established. The following chapter has been designed to help managers to gain this necessary knowledge.

As with other generations, the birth years that define the Millennial generation are controversial, ranging from 1981 to 2000 (Armour 2005). Some believe this generation begins in 1977 because that is when birth rates increased for the first time in ten years (Mui 2001). However, more narrow definitions frequently list 1980 to 1993 (Aschoff 2006). Despite the definition, researchers generally say that Millennials have now been in the workforce for four years (Gerdes 2007a). However, for the purposes of this book, the Millennial Generation will be defined as those who were born between 1981 and 2000.

In total, this generation is nearly 80 million members strong (Gerdes 2006). They have been known for their close relationships with parents and educators, as well as their idealism that mirrored that of the Baby Boomers (Underwood 2007). Regardless of their similarities with both the Baby Boomers and Gen X, some believe they are most similar to the GI, or Great Generation, that their grandparents belonged to because of a similar "can-do attitude of the World War II generation" (Bounds 2000). Others argue that this bunch could be "Gen X on fast forward with self-esteem" (Tulgan & Martin 2001). No matter which generation they are compared to, they have significant characteristics that define them as a unique group.

The "first-wave" Millennials, those aged 16 to 25, have shared commonalities in home-life, education, work, and interests (Jayson 2006). Unlike members of Generation X, parents have been available and involved in the lives of Millennials. This active parenting role led to a strong support system and an overscheduled childhood (Gerdes 2006). The increasing parental influence and empowerment also leads many Millennials to believe that they will be financially successful in the future (Mui 2001). Despite strong parental involvement, many students who have left home say they remain close to their parents because they like the close relationship, which contradicts the precedents set by previous generations (Jayson 2006).

Members of the Millennial generation also grew up with increased education and diversity that led to a more tolerant atmosphere. Sixty percent of 18- to 29-year-olds say they have dated a member of a different race. That same percentage of teens also say they have friends of different races. The generation itself is the most diverse demographically with one-third belonging to a minority (Trunk 2007). Similarly, they are more educated than past generations with twice as many undergraduates enrolled in college and more students intending to pursue graduate degrees (Jayson 2006).

Technology has made a prominent impact on all aspects of this generation's lives since birth, which has led to nicknames such as Speeders, Internet Generation, and Generation Next (Bounds 2000). They have been raised with computers, cell phones, and video games unlike any preceding generations. Cathilea Robinett, the Executive Director of the Center for Digital Government and Center for Digital Education said, "They were born with technology, they don't know any other reality. They have been interactive from day one" (Lane 2006).

Technological advances have driven their ability to multi-task (Trunk 2007). Their online networking abilities have also aided in the development of skills that employers require, such as computer skills and teamwork (Gerdes 2006). However, the epidemic use of MySpace, Facebook, YouTube, and reality TV has led to criticism of Millennials being "attention [hounds]" ("Gen Yers changing" 2007). Online social networking sites are greatly to blame for the excessively self-consumed focus because many older generations argue they are simply utilized for the gain of personal attention. Yet, members of this generation are quick to argue that they also promote social causes and ideas (Swann 2007).

A study that concluded in 2006 reported Millennials as having the highest recorded scores on the Narcissistic Personal

Inventory with a 30 percent increase since its creation in 1982. It reported Millennials lacked empathy for others and valued self over relationships. William Strauss, the author of *Millennials Rising: The Next Great Generation* suggests this is misrepresented. He said, "As in any generation you will find examples of self-oriented behavior, but we should not let youthful ambition be mischaracterized as narcissism." (Swann 2007)

Along with ambition, opponents are quick to mention the numerous charity programs and causes that Millennials continue to assist. For example, one of the most popular videos on MySpace last year belonged to Invisible Children, an awareness program that assists children in war-torn Uganda. This cause was not only developed by Millennials, but also is solely run by members of this young generation. Altruism has also led to alternative spring breaks at many colleges and universities where students spend their free time assisting causes and those less fortunate. In a survey of freshmen it was demonstrated that over 66 percent felt it was essential or very important to help others, which was the highest percentage in 25 years (Jayson 2006).

While interested in world events, members of Generation Y do not seek information from traditional news media. Similarly, while becoming civically engaged is popular, it is not believed to be true for voting or politics. Others argue that members of this generation do possess interest in politics, but that interest is not typically party specific, which limits organized involvement (Aschoff 2006).

Despite the limited involvement, Millennials possess increased trust in institutions and teamwork, most similarly to that of the

GI Generation. They claim to "favor government intervention to solve problems," including environmental and social issues. Perhaps this has largely influenced their belief that they can run government in more productive ways with a "get-it-done" type attitude (Swann 2007). Many Millennials also choose to contribute to society through their career choices, which allow government agencies and non-profits to excel in recruiting (Gerdes 2006). The significant perspective change of Generation Y is believed to have developed because they "don't feel cheated by society" like members of Generation X (Bounds 2000).

This is a generation afflicted with Columbine shootings, attempted presidential impeachments and scandal, yet they also saw the stabilization of online companies. They have experienced the initial shock and vulnerability of 9/11, as well as the patriotism that followed. They know both the fury and fallout of Hurricane Katrina. Recent events have provided this generation with a lowered sense of safety, yet they remain strong in their conviction that they can do good.

Current conditions have allowed Millennials to delay making many serious decisions. As "boomerang kids" they live with parents after college. They also may tryout new jobs or cities while postponing serious relationships and marriage (Underwood 2007). These "traditional measures of childhood" are delayed, in part by education, as only 37 percent graduate college in four years (Jayson 2006). Although, there may be something to be said for not jumping into things, because the commitment and value of marriage appears to be increasing ("Gen Yers changing" 2007). Additionally, there has been a decline in crime and sexual risk-taking over the past 15 years, which are typically behaviors associated with adolescents (Swann 2007).

In the workplace, many have categorized Millennials as "a generation that expects the world at 27 years old" (Mui 2001). As economic decreases in recent years have slightly limited Millennials' expectations, more of them acknowledge that they must work their way up the corporate ladder (Chen 2001). However, the nature of this generation is not inclined toward corporate climbing (Aschoff 2006). Instead, a practical approach and individual definitions of success allow them to find their niche (Hulett 2006).

That same practicality has influenced top majors for this generation to include business, engineering, and medical fields (Aschoff 2006). Their sound choices make 82 percent of job-seekers confident they will find a job they want, according to Wet Feet Research and Consulting (Gerdes 2006). Fifty percent also believe they will have fulfilling careers (Aschoff 2006). Upon entering new positions, they do not only want to see the short-term, but also the long-term possibilities that await them (Hulett 2006).

Members of this 'Internet Generation' are information gatherers because they are used to having the world—or at least the World Wide Web at their fingertips, no matter the time of day. They are technologically proficient, success oriented, feedback driven, and want a quick, deliberate impact (Gerdes 2006). Responsibility is a top priority along with the challenge it brings. They want opportunity to explore, followed by team analysis (Tulgan & Martin 2001). Technologies that older generations once found vital, such as voicemail, have now become trivial and "a waste of time" (Aschoff 2006).

As Millennials change workplace dynamics, expectations are also called into question. Increased praise and constructive feedback are not just welcomed but required. After all, this generation received more coddling and input from parents throughout their entire lives. The heightened expectations are not hypocritical as they run full circle, including both the employer and themselves (Gerdes 2007a).

The changes this generation has observed, like outsourcing and corporate restructuring, have led to the expectation that Millennials will undoubtedly work for more than one company (Rushowy 2007). They will likely job-hop. Similarly, they are not in a hurry to begin the career paths that Baby Boomers fought to obtain. They are willing to take unrelated jobs or travel after graduation, searching for new experiences (Jayson 2006). "They simply aren't prepared to mortgage their lives to the company" (Braid 2007).

A Universum survey revealed that the number one goal of people belonging to Generation Y was to lead a balanced life (Gerdes 2006). While striving for that balance, Millennials often question typical workplace expectations, such as standard work hours. Psychology Professor Ruth F. Fassinger, Ph.D, also notes that women in this generation are more forthcoming regarding parental obligations (Dittmann 2005). Raised in an environment that promoted self-esteem, they are not afraid to challenge corporate norms. This group values leisure time above all else and might be better suited as members of an increasingly contingent workforce where they make their own decisions about how much time to commit to work and leisure and receive payment on a piecework or hourly pay structure.

Unlike past generations, financial security ranks third, reflecting their delay in choosing to purchase homes and start families (Gerdes 2006). For this generation, the typical college graduate earned a degree two years ago and moved back in with parents upon graduation. They will take a temporary job that becomes permanent, allowing them to move in with roommates (Jayson 2006). Yet, they will remain close with family and friends. All the while, the only phone line they maintain for communication is a cellular one. The significant differences observed in contrast to those before them make Millennials "the group to watch."

As this new generation has entered the workforce, certain myths and inaccurate perceptions have developed about them. While there may be grains of truth in each of these myths, overall, they are not an accurate portrayal of this generational cohort.

This group undeniably has different perspectives than generations past on both work and home-life; however, Millennials are not unrealistic about the fact that they will have to work their way up the corporate ladder in order to achieve their career aspirations. Understanding that while initial perceptions often times result from some sort of truth, they are not always accurate. It is important for managers to be aware that while first impressions may be somewhat legitimate, it does not always provide insight into who Millennials truly are.

It has been suggested that Millennials have a much more pragmatic outlook on life than the generations that preceded them. This generational cohort has "reported themselves to be the least optimistic of [the other generational cohorts present in the workforce]." It is predicted that the extreme realism Millennials have developed resulted from the strong presence of media throughout their lives which exposed them to world events, present and past, on a much more frequent and in-depth level than previous generations experienced. Moreover, "it may be that this generation has witnessed past generations (for example, their parents and grandparents) fail or not meet their goals and therefore are more cautious and worried about their own future" (Wong et al. 2008). The observation of the trials and tribulations their parents and grandparents had to face in their lifetimes likely contributes to the apprehension Millennials feel since the possibility of failure seems all too familiar and possible.

The pragmatic viewpoint Millennials possess helps to explain their proactive approach to career development. As a result of watching older generations experience layoffs and uncertain futures in terms of job security, Millennials place a great deal of value on fully developing diverse skill sets that will ensure their marketability in the long run (Westerman & Yamamura 2007). It has been observed that "rather than passively relying on employers to take responsibility for employee career development, younger generation employees, [namely Millennials], are more likely to take a more active role in their career planning and execution." If companies are unable to provide opportunities for Millennials to fully build their skill sets, high levels of dissatisfaction will result (Westerman & Yamamura 2007).

This diverse generation is quite complex and fully understanding them will require continued research and analysis. As this generation progresses in the workplace, different characteristics will be revealed as they transgress through the different phases of their careers.

③ Expectations and Values

Employees' expectations and values are directly related to their success in the workplace. Because of the diverse spread of generations currently in the workforce, expectations and values vary considerably from each employee to the next. The best managers will take into full consideration the characteristics and life experiences that shape employees' behavior, including their generational influences. Although it is a common perception that employees' expectations surround extrinsic variables, intrinsic motivators have shown to be equally as important (Westerman & Yamamura 2007). Employers must realize how important it is to understand their employees are a diverse and complex group of people possessing different needs and wants.

Studies have revealed that one's generation can be a large determinant in the development of expectations and values for careers and workplaces. Smola and Sutton speculate that a generation's personality, beliefs, and concerns regarding authority are determined by "their values and beliefs about organizations, their work ethic, why and how they work and their goals and aspirations for their work life," which are often developed from the social influences that affect each individual's respective generation (Wong et al. 2008). Additionally, it has been proposed that each generation develops specific and unique inclinations and attributes that establish their beliefs and aspirations in regard to the workplace (Wong et al. 2008).

The point at which a person is, in terms of their career stage, can be extremely influential in the determination of their expectations and values. As each generation enters into a more mature stage of their career, certain values that were once deemed to be very important become less of a priority. For example, a younger generation that was studied "placed more importance on status than the older group...[since] the career stage of the older group may [have] provide[d] status so they no longer [felt] that status [was] a priority as it provides visibility which aids [career] progression and marketability" (Cennamo & Gardner 2008).

Although there are significant differences in the value each generation places on various aspects of the work environment, there are some common expectations and values that all generations share. Flexibility in the workplace is one such value. Whether flexibility is needed to care for aging parents, young children, or for personal time to further one's education, it remains a consistent value. Overall, it promotes a greater work-life balance for all employees. Companies that incorporate flexible work schedules as a way to promote work-life balance with benefits such as paternity leave are seeing positive reactions from their employees (Shellenbarger 2007). Likewise, more employers are eliminating set hours in favor of alternative schedule options including working from home or other locations. Since this can result in new difficulties, including decreased team interactivity, some companies require a designated day per week that all employees are on-site.

In addition to aspects of the workforce that are important cross-generationally, there are certain expectations and values shared by different pairs of generations. As research presented in the *Harvard Business Review* has proved, Baby Boomers and members of the Millennial generation place similar worth on common things. Correlations have been established between every other generation (Howe & Strauss 2007). Among the generations currently present in the workforce, this ties together Baby Boomers and Millennials, as well as Generation X with the Silent Generation (Howe & Strauss 2007). The result of these cross-generational links is that these groups will likely possess some shared values and expectations.

GENERATIONAL SPECIFIC EXPECTATIONS AND VALUES

While understanding each of the generations currently present in the workforce is important, the majority of applicable research and information presented focuses on Baby Boomers, Generation X, and Millennials since they are the most salient groups at this point in time. Additionally, because these three generations are expected to remain in the workplace for a significant amount of time, they will continue to be studied.

GI GENERATION

The GI (or Traditionalist) generation grew up during a time when rewards came to those who obeyed defined structures and rules and worked hard for significant lengths of time. This generation has core values that center around dedication/

sacrifice, hard work, conformity, law and order, respect for authority, delayed reward, duty before pleasure, and an adherence to the rules. As a result of their upbringing, members of this generation possess the expectations and beliefs that institutions should provide security and promote employees who have proven themselves over time. Additionally, they believe that demonstrating loyalty to the organization, following management instruction, and respecting co-workers and superiors should lead to them to success within the organization (Patota, Schwartz, & Schwartz 2007).

BABY BOOMERS

Baby Boomers were taught to value optimism, involvement, and personal growth. They are team oriented and concerned with health and wellness. In terms of expectations and values, Baby Boomers uphold the core beliefs of the Prophet archetype. Growing up during a period of rejuvenation contributed greatly to this group's optimistic beliefs and its drive to pursue goals (Patota, Schwartz, & Schwartz 2007). Their focus tends to center around work in order to ensure a better future for themselves and their children. Although it is a widely accepted belief that Baby Boomers have a high level of status value, studies have shown the desire for tenure and advancement within a company is no longer as prominent as it used to be. It is believed that this may be a result of the career stage in which Baby Boomers generally reside, making these aspirations ones that have already been satisfied (Cennamo & Gardner 2008). Also related to career stage, this generation has reached a point at which they no longer have a strong need to network and socialize as they once did (Wong et al. 2008). Because this generation has developed such a career-oriented existence, they may often times find it difficult to balance work and home-life and to nurture relationships both at work and at home (Cennamo & Gardner 2008).

GENERATION X

The members of Generation X were some of the least protected children out of all four generations. As a result, they have developed core values that encompass team work, thinking globally, accepting diversity, and the ever constant characteristic of self-reliance. In direct contrast to Traditionalists who worked to live, Generation X requires more of a work-life balance. They possess a strong belief in hard work, but they also see the need for developing a life outside of work (Patota, Schwartz, & Schwartz 2007). Members of Generation X "have more commitment to their careers than to their organizations and may prefer [those] which value skills development, productivity, and work-life balance rather than status and tenure" (Cennamo & Gardner 2008).

This is the first generation to truly integrate the technology of computers into their everyday work function. They hold an expectation for their organizations to promote based on ability rather than seniority and to provide security through the benefit of diverse work options instead of through longevity with the company. Additionally, this group has opinions that they expect to be considered and valued within the organization (Patota, Schwartz, & Schwartz 2007).

MILLENNIALS

During the short period that Millennials have been present in the workforce, it has become apparent that this generation has developed its own set of unique values and expectations. Among the many that have been observed thus far, optimism, civic duty, confidence, achievement, social ability, morality, street smarts, and the importance of diversity are at the core of what this group deems important. They excel at multi-tasking, working in groups, and feel the need to have a structured environment in which they have a close relationship with their supervisors. Although the Millennial generation falls into a different archetypal categorization than the Traditionalists, they relate closely and have strong communication with this older generation (Patota, Schwartz, & Schwartz 2007). This substantial tie between the two generations may be due to the fact that both place high value on hard work and view structure as an integral and important part of the workplace.

As the Millennial generation has begun to infiltrate the workforce, an enormous amount of assumptions have been made about this young group of professionals. While there may be some truth behind the myths, many of the common perceptions are not accurate. Contrary to popular belief, younger employees are not opposed to working long hours, provided flexible options are offered (Gerdes 2006). For example, Millennials expect the opportunity to work flexibly outside traditional hours through the options provided by new technologies such as telecommunication and virtual meetings (Lane 2006).

Corporations are quickly discovering that flexibility is of the utmost importance to Millennials. In terms of flexible work scheduling, employees in their twenties often want the ability to further their education. Research has shown that Millennials also place substantial value on being provided opportunities to continue their education, inside and outside of the classroom, as they correlate learning closely to career development (D'Amato & Herzfeldt 2008). When companies provide the flexibility that allows their employees to pursue continued education, they satisfy this important value of the Millennial generation.

Specific to the Millennial generation, self-perception of continued education often times differs greatly from realized educational achievements (Twenge & Campbell 2008). For example, in a study cited by Twenge & Campbell, it was reported that "more than half of recent high school students (51 percent) predicted that they would earn graduate or professional degrees even though only 9 percent of 25–34-year-old high school graduates actually hold these degrees" (2008). Comparatively, "in 1976, only half as many (27 percent) predicted this outcome...during the same period, the percentage of high school students who predicted that they would be working in a professional job by age 30 also increased, from 41 percent to 63 percent, in reality, only 18 percent of high school graduates ages 25 to 34 in both eras worked at professional jobs" (Twenge & Campbell 2008). It is likely that the influences imposed upon generations that fall into the Hero archetype contribute greatly to the largely unrealistic expectations that individuals in this group develop.

Millennials have a perception that careers are the accumulation of "multiple jobs across multiple organizations." As a result of the layoffs and lack of job security in the recent past, the idea that lifelong career paths with one corporation are possible may be skewed. In strict contrast to the Baby Boomer generation, Millennials feel the need to socialize on a regular basis in order to advance their careers and fully develop relationships through networking. Their observation of preceding generations has led Millennials to believe they are more likely to be hired and advance in their careers as a result of the personal connections they make, rather than exclusively based on their skills, abilities, or educational achievements (Twenge & Campbell 2008).

It has been concluded that Millennials value "work/life balance, life styles, career development and overseas travel more than other generations.[and] may be the most adaptable yet in terms of technological skills and has been said to value intrinsic aspects of work such as mentoring and training in order to remain marketable" (Cennamo & Gardner 2008).

Millennials possess a very clear idea of what they expect from their employers. In an ideal world, a Millennial would work for an employer that is capable of balancing optimism with realism in terms of the company's relations with employees and the outside world. However, despite this generation's idealistic views, they are unwilling to forfeit their personal job security in order for these desires to be realized ("Generation Y" 2008).

④ Building Relationships

In terms of relationship building, it is important to fully understand the competencies of each generation. Combining competency understanding with the information about each generation's strengths, weaknesses, expectations, and values allows individuals within organizations to build productive and positive relationships. Research conducted by Patota, Schwartz, and Schwartz has shown there are eight emblematic competencies that define how people of all generations function in the workplace (2007). These eight competencies include developing people, communication skills, team work, customer service, organizational objectives, managing resources, problem solving, and valuing diversity (Patota, Schwartz, & Schwartz 2007).

These competencies are substantially similar to many of the values and expectations that each generation possesses. The first competency, developing people, "promotes performance of others by hiring effectively, providing clear feedback, mentoring, and appropriately using talents." Each generation has a unique viewpoint on appropriate promotion methods and feedback requirements. Because some generational beliefs are in direct opposition to one another, it can be difficult for productive relationships to be formed. For example, Baby Boomers and members of Generation X have opposing views on many things. For example, when forging relationships between these two groups, there may be crucial differences in beliefs about appropriate promotion practices among other organizational practices (Patota, Schwartz, & Schwartz 2007).

Baby Boomers value hard work and continued commitment to the betterment of the organization, while Generation Xers are more concerned with personal career development. In direct correlation to these values, Baby Boomers feel that promotion should be largely based on longevity with the organization, while members of Generation X believe employees should be promoted based on ability and aptitude. Such disagreement in core beliefs creates an environment in which each generation focuses on these differences, perceiving them as weaknesses instead of recognizing the potential strengths that may exist. It has been found that "as a result of these conflicting beliefs, a Baby Boomer in power may focus only on the perceived weakness, such as lack of dedication to the job, and overlook the significant strengths of the Generation Xer, i.e., the ability to accept and even accelerate change...[and] in contrast, a Generation Xer in power, who wants a 'fun' workplace, may find the seriousness and dedication of the Baby Boomer employee to be oppressive and incomprehensible" (Patota, Schwartz, & Schwartz 2007).

A person exhibiting the next important competency, communication skills, has the ability to "skillfully present thoughts in individual and group situations." Although this competency is relatively straightforward, it is among one of the biggest contributors to relationship growth and/

or limitation. Regardless of the generation a person belongs to, they may not have strong communication skills, which can hinder productivity. Individuals with the ability to communicate effectively with others have a significant edge on peers without strong skills.

In today's business world where a strong focus on collaboration exists, team work is a significant competency for building relationships in the workplace. An individual who demonstrates a strong understanding of teamwork requirements "establishes and motivates teams, provides a sense of purpose and cohesiveness to a group, [and] delivers results with cross functional teams" (Patota, Schwartz, & Schwartz 2007). Younger generations tend to work better in a group setting which leads to the prediction that the workplace will migrate towards more team work and group-centered projects. Thus, the importance of developing skills or competencies that are conducive to group environments is becoming increasingly essential.

Another competency that translates across generations is customer service. While not everyone is capable of effective interaction with others, those that possess a high level of skill for this competency will "provide a high degree of satisfaction for the customer, exceeding expectations" (Patota, Schwartz, & Schwartz 2007). Regardless of industry or job description, customer service skills play a crucial role in developing a positive reputation and establishing lasting relationships with customers.

Next, professionals with the ability to understand and implement the importance of organizational objectives, will be able to "define a clear and compelling image of the organization's goals and what it stands for and make personal sacrifices for the good of the organization" (Patota, Schwartz, & Schwartz 2007). This competency is predominantly determined by the industry and/or company in which an individual works. While this may not be an innate ability, it can be learned over time and different people may have a greater aptitude to acquire this critical skill.

Managing resources is another competency not necessarily correlated with all of the generations. People with the ability to manage resources well will "manage expenditures to reduce costs and improve quality [and will] search for ways of doing things [more effectively]" (Patota, Schwartz, & Schwartz 2007). Reducing costs while maintaining or improving quality is one of the most important priorities for effectively managing resources since companies around the world are constantly striving to be as efficient as possible.

The competency that involves the capability to effectively solve problems is often times an innate quality, but can also be learned. An employee who possesses this ability is actively involved in the "develop[ment of] creative ideas and solutions that improve the organization's service, quality, revenues, and profits" (Patota, Schwartz, & Schwartz 2007). Innovation is the heart of almost every leading company's culture, so the talent to think creatively is of immeasurable value.

The final competency, valuing diversity, can be attributed to those who "create an atmosphere of valuing and accepting others [and who] listen and act [based] on the concerns, interests, and feelings of others" (Patota, Schwartz, & Schwartz 2007). This chapter has focused mainly on diversity in age. However, it is crucial to have a well-rounded appreciation for all facets of diversity ranging from ethnicity to education level to socioeconomic status. The workforce as it exists today is an extremely diverse population, making the importance of valuing and understanding the strengths in existing differences vital to the success of any individual or company.

In terms of building successful and positive relationships within the workplace, possessing several of the emblematic competencies is essential to individuals and companies as a whole. Individual organizations will have their own set of critical competencies; however, the general competencies discussed provide a strong baseline upon which every business can expand. Building strong relationships internally and externally is key to a company's ability to manage its "services, products, people, and other resources" (Patota, Schwartz, & Schwartz 2007).

Millennials often use technology such as cell phones, iPods, instant messaging, and social networking sites to maintain relationships outside of the work environment. Reliance on electronics promotes communication, but also contributes to the lack of non-verbal communication and personal interaction (Jayson 2006). While this is true for relationships outside the office, it is also true for the business environment. Technology has its drawbacks since it removes the necessity of interacting through face-to-face personal communication. It is hard to impress upon the Millennial generation that technology is not always the best way to communicate (Gale 2007). Use of technology such as email in the workplace, provides for possibilities of misinterpretation, particularly by different generations, because of differing formalities and norms. This may expose intergenerational conflict and cause working relationship problems that may undermine potential products or services (Dittmann 2005).

Technological communications are not the only issues that arise between co-workers. Studies have shown that "more than 70 percent of older employees are dismissive of younger workers' abilities." Nearly half indicate younger employees are dismissive of their older counterparts (Armour 2005). Hidden in the numbers, a generational gap may in fact represent a power struggle (Frazier 2007). Baby Boomers have a very "play-by-the-rules approach" that younger workers do not understand (Dittmann 2005). Similarly, Generation X often views Millennials as entitled or arrogant because they think "they're doing you a favor by working for you" (Mui 2001). Generation Xers and Millennials have distinct differences despite a slight age difference. Differences between Generation X and the Millenial generation were largely influenced by economics and cultural differences. Many Millennials do not want to be associated with Generation X because they view them as complainers, negative, and slackers. Baby Boomers often find it easier to mentor Millennials because of their parental-like nature. Meanwhile, Generation Xers may have a difficult time finding the most effective way to interact with the Millennials because of the preconceived notions about the group (Gerdes 2007b).

Millennials have high expectations of employers and expect to be treated as equals upon entering the workforce. Employers argue that a degree is not enough to warrant this level of respect because experience, which is gained with age, enhances abilities." Application of knowledge requires lots of simple common sense, and you get that by critical observations and experiences on the job" (Gale 2007). Some young workers say they even lie about their age to co-workers to attain greater respect (Armour 2005). Meanwhile, organizational behaviorists insist that honest communications will always bring a better outcome when working with one another (Dittmann 2005).

Communication through both listening and expression is important among all generations. Baby Boomers often say they feel tossed aside or underappreciated by the overwhelming excitement for change that Millennials bring. While some Millennials may appear ungrateful, others grasp the importance of what past generations have done. Katie Yontz, a young employee in an advertising agency, explained her awe over the fact that on the day she was born, her employers began their company. She feels they "have so much experience and insight" (Frazier 2007). In the ideal intergenerational team, individuals are empowered to explore ideas, value different views and learning processes, define roles of team members, accommodate each other, listen actively, support sharing expertise, recognize hard work from all, and keep meetings enjoyable with humor (Dittmann 2005).

Together these groups can be highly effective. A younger employee's desire to change things with new and creative ideas complements the older generations' knowledge of history and processes which creates a positive work environment (Hymowitz 2007). Similarly, young employees frequently know how to use technology to its full capability, allowing them to multi-task and communicate effectively (Gale 2007). Many researchers suggest that older generations can learn a great deal from observing how the younger generations communicate and allowing them to "teach the teacher" in a reversal of traditional age-based roles.

Through workshops that find a balance between procedures and creative flexibility, some generational consultants strive to "blend generations' work ethics" (Dittmann 2005). In an effort to boost productivity and increase employee retention, some companies are reaping the benefits of implementing training and work-sharing programs for employees. By pairing new employees with established agents, no one ever works alone. This structure provides a partnership between two diverse generations that promotes assistance and relationship building (Berfield 2007).

⑤ Psychological Contracts

Creating workplace partnerships among generations can be difficult. Knowing the common ground that exists between two individuals is problematic at best and can be summed into the concept of the "psychological contract." Increasingly at work, managers, line workers, executives, and support staff all struggle to define the boundaries of their roles and the expectations of their superiors. With the presence of multiple generations in today's workplace it is paramount to understand and define the expectations of individuals at work. With our focus on Millennials, this distinction takes on special importance. A group that values leisure time above all else, craves praise and attention and seeks to meet the needs of their supervisors to move up the corporate ladder, an intact psychological contract is imperative.

The concept of the psychological contract dates back to Argyris (1960) who mentioned the concept in passing as he discussed other facets of organizational justice. Levinson et al. (1962) offered an early definition of the psychological contract as the "unwritten (work) agreement (and the) sum of the mutual (work) expectations." These definitions are problematic at best and have given rise to several revisions over the years (Herriot & Pemberton 1995, Schein 1965, 1990). It is generally agreed that the psychological contract plays an important, if not crucial role in shaping employee behavior in the workplace (Anderson & Schalk 1998). However, as a relatively new development in organizational research, many facets of the psychological contract have come under scrutiny and have been the subject of debate. Scholars have debated measurement, the correct unit of analysis, the added value of psychological contract research as well as the nomenclature, as many feel the term "contract" is an improper metaphor when discussing this concept.

As a result, when researchers discuss a "psychological contract" the concept is still, to some extent, nebulous. To this end, any discussion of the psychological contract must specifically outline what is intended to comprise the contract (Rousseau 1998). To date, a widely accepted definition has emerged from Rousseau (1995) who attempted to remove levels issues by defining the psychological contract as:

> *The individual's beliefs about mutual obligations, in the context of the relationship between employer and employee.*

By placing the construct in a unilateral individual level of analysis questions of operationalization for empirical study has become an issue of great concern. Moreover, results reported in all previous studies have been examined without attention to the potential for cultural and generational differences in interpretation of the psychological contract. As evident in other realms of organizational research, cultures and further different groups such as generational groupings, can differ in their behavior, interpretations, and attitudes toward work (Chrobot-Mason & Leslie 2003, Greenberg 2001, Mueller & Clarke 1998, Sanchez & Brock 1996, Thomas & Au 2000). Increasingly, scholars have investigated the impact of contract fairness as well as the benefit derived from the intact psychological contract. Portwood & Miller (1979) in an early study are among the first to report job satisfaction and evaluations of employee work behavior as positively correlated with their measure of what they term "organization contract compliance." "Organization contract compliance" is quite similar to what is today characterized as psychological contract fulfillment.

PSYCHOLOGICAL CONTRACT FAIRNESS

Psychological contract violation, or perceptions of an unfair psychological contract, have been shown to afford many adverse results (Coyle-Shapiro & Kessler 2000, Cavanaugh & Noe 1999, Lewis-McClear & Taylor 1997, Masterson 2001, Rousseau & Anton 1988, Rousseau & Anton 1991, Turnley & Feldman 1999). Violation of the psychological contract occurs when an employee perceives that the organization has failed to fulfill one or more of its "contractual obligations." Psychological contract violations come in two forms: reneging or incongruence. Reneging occurs when the organization knowingly breaks a promise to the employee, either on purpose or because of unforeseen circumstances. In contrast, incongruence is marked by the difference in perceptions of the individual and the organization, for example the organization might believe that it has lived up to its commitments, but the individual perceives the organization has failed to meet their expectations (Rousseau 1995).

In most cases the dependent variable of interest was the overall "fairness" evaluation score assigned to each individual's psychological contract. By such an operational definition, it is conceivable that participants will include varying degrees of contract violation corresponding to the levels of contract fairness. In these cases, the contract has not necessarily been broken, yet negative outcomes of violation can still be evident (Coyle-Shapiro & Kessler 2000, Robinson & Rousseau 1994). The results of psychological contract violation range from outcomes such as negative impact on employees' work behaviors and attitudes to voluntary turnover (Coyle-Shapiro & Kessler 2000, Rousseau & McLean Parks 1993) to predicting discretionary service behaviors (Blancero & Johnson 2001). Conversely, the intact psychological contract has predicted many potential benefits. Researchers have shown that individuals with intact contracts have high levels of organizational commitment, extra-role behavior that promotes effective functioning of the organization (Organizational Citizenship Behavior—OCB), productivity, and job satisfaction (Coyle-Shapiro & Kessler 2000, Cavanaugh & Noe 1999, Rousseau & Anton 1988, Lewis-McClear & Taylor 1997, Masterson 2001, Robinson & Rousseau 1994, Rousseau & Anton 1991, Turnley & Feldman 1999).

MEASURING THE PSYCHOLOGICAL CONTRACT

Scholars normally align themselves with one of several camps ranging from benevolent servants of Rousseau's concepts, to those who find the concept questionable at best. The bulk of the controversy has focused on issues surrounding the use of the "legal metaphor" (in reference to "contract" terminology) and measurement issues. Some individuals from the legal profession have contended that the psychological contract is not a true "contract" in that the implicit nature does not allow for the requisite "meeting of the minds" (Guest 1998). Measurement issues have surrounded the "what to measure?" question, as some scholars have pursued content of the psychological contract, some have explored features of the psychological contract, and yet others have explored evaluation of the psychological contract.

DYNAMIC NATURE OF THE PSYCHOLOGICAL CONTRACT

Also of note is the dynamic nature of the psychological contract. Changes in the contract over time can be related to fairness, however unagreed changes could have positive outcomes while still terming the contract as "violated." For example, one's beliefs about an employer's obligations when they begin work will differ greatly from their beliefs after one year, two years, or three years of employment (Robinson, Kraatz & Rousseau 1994, Rousseau & Anton 1988, Rousseau 1990, Rousseau & Anton 1991). Robinson, Kraatz & Rousseau (1994) found that during the first two years of employment, employees felt they owed less to their employers and the employers owed the employees more. In the end, it was shown that an employer's failure to fulfill its commitments is significantly associated with decline in some types of employee commitments.

While Guest (1998), Rousseau (1998) and Rousseau & Tijoriwala (1996) all posit that the "greatest good" might arise from research in content-oriented research, it seems that features and moreover evaluation of the contract are the concepts of true value. The problematic idiosyncratic nature of the work agreement does not lend itself to an overarching taxonomy of psychological contract content. Rousseau (2001) and Rousseau & Schalk (2001) demonstrate this predicament as they have begun to propose theories of the "idiosyncratic work agreement" going so far as to state that the more idiosyncratic or individualized the agreement becomes, the more positive the outcomes (such as commitment, satisfaction, OCBs, and so on) will become. Further work in feature-oriented psychological contract research will provide more insight as to how the agreement is communicated, what methods of communication are most beneficial, and so on. In this vein, practicing managers/organizational agents can adapt their method of communication to match that which is associated with positive outcomes. However, evaluation-oriented research can be a most intriguing source of knowledge regarding the psychological contract since it can easily be causally related to individual level outcomes. As an individual-level phenomenon, researchers (and managers) seek to find impact of intact/fair psychological contracts.

CROSS-CULTURAL PSYCHOLOGICAL CONTRACT RESEARCH

As noted earlier, scant research addresses the unique nature of diverse generations working together. This being said, scholars posit that cross-cultural research comes closest to replicating the needed investigation of cross-generational issues at work. Hence, investigating cross-cultural psychological contract research might inform our understanding of the psychological contract cross-generationally.

A recent wave of psychological contract research has surrounded "cross-cultural issues" related to the psychological contract (Rousseau & Tijoriwala 1996, Rousseau & Schalk 2001). The focus of this research has also been on content of the psychological contract, but in this case, across cultures and can be extrapolated across generational groupings. Thomas & Au (2000) address cultural variation in the psychological contract. Most of their differences are theoretical and relate only to content of the contract for Asian workers. Their study was based on the perceptions (evaluation) of fairness cross-culturally. They conclude that the psychological contract differs across cultures. By extrapolation, perhaps less-developed countries or traditionally repressed groups are less likely to report their contract as violated/unfair. Or conversely, due to hypersensitivity are more likely to report their psychological contract as violated/unfair. It seems interesting to examine the perceptions of individuals' cross-cultural base. Through this line of research, evidence of lingering bias, bigotry, or feelings of inferiority in the workplace may be evidenced.

Many scholars have done meaningful empirical and theoretical work in psychological contracts that with cross-cultural samples. Robinson & Morrison (2000) examined psychological contract fairness through the lens of contextual influences; they found a significant increase in violation reports in instances of low organizational performance, lack of formal socialization process, lack of or inappropriate job previews, increased number of job options/offers (before choosing the job studied), and in instances where the employee has a history of psychological contract violation in previous employments. Two findings of Robinson & Morrisson (2000) suggest that individual differences do, in fact, predict psychological contract fairness, where different individual circumstances also predict such behavior. Cavanaugh & Noe (1999) examined the importance of differing interpretations of the relational component of the psychological contract. They found significant results in terms of fairness reports. They concluded that individuals have different interpretations of their relational psychological contract. Additionally, Turnley & Feldman (2000) examined the relationship between job satisfaction and reports of psychological contract fairness. Turnley & Feldman (2000) showed that job dissatisfaction leads to reports of psychological contract fairness reports and concluded that further examination of the source of psychological contract fairness is well warranted.

In a theoretical examination of note, Morrisson & Robinson (1997) presented a model of determinants and characteristics of psychological contract violations, which is similar to the present study. However, the study identified contextual influences and supervisor behaviors while ignoring the potential influence of individual difference variables. Unfortunately, Morrison & Robinson (1997) view the psychological contract from the viewpoint of the organizational/contextual influences ignoring the initial theoretical constraints placed by Rousseau (1995, 1998). Rousseau states that psychological contracts can only be evaluated from the side of the individual. Thus, an examination such as the present study can lend itself to a more theoretical extension of the original intent of psychological contract theory.

Lester, Turnley & Bloodgood (2002) attempted to determine "why" the psychological contract is determined to be violated. They attempt to look at the psychological contract from both the employee and employer perspective. Lester, Turnley & Bloodgood (2002) found that individuals differ in their interpretations of the psychological contract and thus report varying levels of fulfillment. In light of this research it seems that individual differences such as generational membership (GI, Baby Boomer, Gen X, Gen Y, and so on) could also dictate interpretation of the psychological contract. It is important to note that this line of reason dictates not necessarily that strong identity with a culture/group that is not the dominant group will influence sensitivity and fairness.

Wolfe Morrison & Robinson (1997) developed a model of how psychological contract fairness evolves. While their model has yet to be tested empirically, they use theoretical and empirical findings to dictate the following basic process:

Reneging/Incongruence→perceived unmet promise→perceived breach →violation

Of particular interest in this model is the operationalization of incongruence. A key to incongruence is the employment of divergent schemata in the development of opinions about the employment agreement. Wolfe Morrison & Robinson (1997) propose that cultural distance, socialization, and perceived similarity are all issues of divergent schemata employed by individuals.

Additionally, Wolfe Morrison & Robinson (1997) suggest that a "comparison process" moderates the relationship between perceptions of unmet promise and perceived breach of contract. Enumerated in this construct are variables such as self-serving biases (in this case, perceptions of discrimination in order to make sense of one's contract breach) and equity sensitivity.

Evaluation-oriented measures of psychological contracts have been an empirically successful avenue for psychological contract work. While some scholars have taken issue with the operational definitions of "violation" and "fairness," overcoming these issues is not impossible. It seems that more immediate value could be derived from research focusing on how "intact" or "fair" the contract is over time. For example, dynamism of the contract is not evident to the employee "living" the contract everyday. However employees are cognizant of when the contract is violated. These employees cannot specify what contents of the contract are stable, but can report violations. Thus, it seems more fruitful to compare employees in terms of the contextual differences driving the "intact" or "fair" contracts (such as individual differences, country of origin, ethnic background, organizational culture, occupations, level of professionalization, nature of relationships, self-efficacy, work-space layout, embeddedness issues, and so on) and the outcomes of the violated contract (reduction in OCBs, absenteeism, turnover, reduced levels of organizational commitment, interpersonal issues).

By extension, issues with psychological contract fulfillment, violation, and breach are all of paramount importance with regard to Millenials entering the workforce. As expectations shift and these individuals (who value leisure time) strive to make in-roads in the workplace, employers must shift their portion of the psychological contract too. In these cases, mangers and employees from different "cultures" or generations must have some sort of "meeting of the minds" in order to arrive at a mutually agreed upon and acceptable set of employment guidelines. Perhaps the conditions that others see as favorable or "fair" might be judged differently by this group with their unique worldview.

6 Organizational Structure, Culture, and Training

STRUCTURE AND CULTURE

It is vital for employers to understand the psychological implications of a work environment on employees (Westerman & Yamamura 2007). Research has shown that employees working within an environment they feel fits them are more likely to be satisfied with their jobs than ones who feel they are not a fit with their environment (Westerman & Yamamura 2007). The way an employee perceives their organization is largely influenced by their expectations and values.

Designing organizational culture and structure that caters to each of the diverse generations currently working is among one of the biggest challenges any corporation faces. Having a well-rounded knowledge of each generation's expectations and values provides insight into the way companies need to structure themselves in order to be appealing to each unique group and to emerge as a leader for recruitment and retention of employees. The diverse range in age of employees that companies must manage creates the challenge of designing an organizational culture that fosters development and growth of each generation.

Generation X was the first generational cohort that truly adopted the technologies available to them by incorporating them into their everyday lives at work and home. Although Traditionalists and Baby Boomers have adapted to technology when necessary, they generally have been less inclined to readily accept technological advances in the workplace and have been resistant to some technology pushes. Since the Millennials have joined the workforce, the trend towards technology has increased further, and the norm of technologically centered businesses now outweighs the resistance to such changes.

The longevity of careers and extended life expectancy has increased over the past few decades, and it is expected that this trend will continue. As a result, the likelihood of many generations working side by side will continue to increase accordingly. This poses another challenge as managers must continue to educate themselves and their employees on the strengths and weaknesses of each generation. Additionally, designing an organizational culture and structure that reflects the values and expectations of multiple generational cohorts becomes increasingly more difficult in correlation to the rising number of generational groups present in the workforce.

The evolution of organizational culture is moving in a techno-centric direction. As the Traditionalists and Baby Boomers begin to retire from the workforce, organizational culture and structure will need to focus more heavily on technology than ever before. The rapid advance in technology over the past decade is an indication of the exponential growth that will likely result over the next ten years. Technology has truly changed the business world and will continue to affect it on a large scale. Not only will this change the way companies do business, it will also affect the way employees interact with one another.

Emerging trends that are attractive to younger generations may seem inappropriate to some Traditionalists and Baby Boomers since these trends starkly contrast the norms of their generations. As each new generation enters the workforce, the accepted norms and standards of the corporate world change. The most current trends observed that directly affect organizational culture are technology centered. The opportunities to create unique and customized work arrangements have increased immensely with the continued evolution of technology.

In order to attract the most talented up-and-coming employees in the Millennial generation, companies must create an organizational culture and structure that focuses on work-life balance through the provision of unique options. Some of the most popular offerings include flex scheduling, telecommuting, flexible dress code, and opportunity for frequent lateral transfers. Millennials place great value on the balance of work and home-life, thus any options put forth that enable them to create that balance are viewed as extremely attractive. The members of the Millennial generation are not afraid to ask questions and often times prefer their supervisor(s) to act as mentors to them. In addition, they want an open line of communication with their managers and/or supervisors that fosters their professional growth. This young group expects the opportunity to fully develop themselves as well-rounded employees through mentorship programs that allow them to experience many different areas of expertise within the business. Along with mentoring, they require recognition of a job well done and consistent feedback to let them know how they are performing. As great value is placed upon professional development, Millennials yearn for challenging tasks rather than time-filling activities (Hulett 2006).

TRAINING

Training, professional development, and the successful design of work groups are all integral parts of any business. These key elements are contingent upon the attainment of a well-rounded knowledge concerning each generation. In general, managers are responsible for structuring training for their employees in order to ensure employees have the skills and knowledge necessary to successfully perform their job duties.

The first aspect that should be addressed is training. Not only is this the most crucial component that contributes to an employee's ability to perform the basic functions of their job, but it should be considered an ongoing process. Research has shown that employees from every generation desire development. Usually, the longing to further develop professional skills results from "fears about employability or 'marketability' in an uncertain world" (D'Amato & Herzfeldt 2008). "Employers increasingly feel an obligation to train their employees because they understand that continuous development is a necessity" (D'Amato & Herzfeldt 2008). While managers were previously responsible for guiding their employees' professional development, younger generations have taken primary responsibility for this task. Therefore, managers need only provide them with the tools and training necessary for them to further their development individually.

As each generation has its own preferences in terms of learning style, the provision of different options that will successfully reach each generational cohort should be offered. For example, Baby Boomers may prefer learning in a classroom setting, while members of Generation X may utilize online training courses, and Millennials may collaborate via networking blogs (Hymowitz 2007). It can generally be assumed that younger generations will be more open minded to participating in training delivered through new technologies, while older generations may resist such options. However, it remains up to the individual to select the method of learning they prefer, whether or not it matches their generation's preference. Managers must provide options and opportunities for all their employees to learn and develop critical skill sets.

Through a strong understanding of generational characteristics and preferences, managers should be able to effectively design productive and well-balanced work groups. Patota, Schwartz, & Schwartz (2007) have identified a generations/competencies matrix that serves a "key management tool for constructing, managing, and working with teams of different generations for optimizing generational strengths on business projects." The matrix can be viewed at the end of this book.

As with any aspect of managing cross-generationally, training and development and the design of productive and well-balanced work groups are all key elements to the success of any business. If managers are observant of the differences between each generation, their associated preferences, learning styles, as well as the different competencies possessed by individuals, they are likely to be successful in training, aiding with professional development, and the design of effective work groups.

(7) Recruitment and Retention Tactics

Hiring for entry-level positions continues to increase at double-digit percentages (Gerdes 2006). For accounting firms alone, the Sarbanes-Oxley Act has created an unprecedented increase in the need to recruit new graduates. Deloitte estimates there will be a need for 50,000 new employees in the next five years (Gerdes 2007a). This means corporations must be creative in order to recruit effectively in a highly competitive market. Millennials may find that their technical and communication abilities make them desirable candidates for many positions; therefore, companies seeking to hire Millennials should tailor their recruiting strategies to accommodate this mindset (Braid 2007). Until recently, strong job markets have provided the option for Millennials to switch positions on a regular basis and have opened up opportunities for consulting (Mui 2001). Common trends, including the reliance on their parents for housing or financial support, allow Millennials to search for a career rather than accepting positions purely for monetary security (Trunk 2007).

Obviously, pay is not the only motivator for Millennials. The desire for work-life balance requires that companies think outside of the box when recruiting and developing benefits packages. Good reputations, social responsibility, and meaningful work remain priorities for Millennials (Rushowy 2007). For employees aged over 35, top desired traits include safe environment, retirement benefits, health/medical benefits, and a meaningful job (Frazier 2007). Meanwhile, employees aged under 35 most desire compensation or pay, benefits, flexibility, and job security. The distinct difference employers must use to set Millennials apart from individuals in other archetypes and in particular, those who are older, is flexibility.

The best attempts at recruiting Millenials will be posted online and emphasize flexibility (Hulett 2006). Equally important is that companies ensure their recruiting process provides a realistic depiction of what Millennials will experience in the workplace (Gerdes 2007a). For most companies, a popular recruiting tool is the implementation of internship programs. More than half of the hires for six of the 2006 "Best Places to Launch a Career" were former interns for their respective company (Gerdes 2006). Internships allow companies to identify strong job candidates and provide them with substantial experiences and training. Companies and Millennials benefit from this type of program because it allows both to discover whether or not expectations align. By providing hands-on experience and increasing responsibility, companies will satisfy Millennials on various extrinsic and intrinsic levels.

Rather than focusing on specific college degrees, top companies desire traits including communication, leadership, and analytical skills, a high grade point average (GPA), and a strong work ethic. They also consider work experience, references, entrepreneurial spirit, and a fun-loving attitude as crucial characteristics. Companies want to "lure the best by getting them young" (Braid 2007). *Business Week's* 2006 "Best Place to Launch a Career" was the Walt Disney Company because of their well-known on-campus recruiting presence, sound benefits, and integrative, teamwork atmosphere (Gerdes 2006). They provide unique opportunities to employees and the fast-paced business environment Millennials desire. Disney excels greatly in recruiting because of brand recognition as well as offering an environment with quick promotions, excitement, and instantaneous impact. In order to attract Millennials, more companies will need to align their business-hiring strategies with those of corporate leaders such as Disney when seeking Millennial college graduates.

The competitive atmosphere to attain Millennial candidates has increased the importance of company flexibility. New recruiting campaigns may be risky and costly, but they pay off when they bring in the best and brightest candidates. Creativity has become a necessity in terms of advertising for both permanent positions and internship opportunities. The corporate traits Millennials admire have been incorporated into many recruiting slogans. After 20 years, the US Army changed its "Be All You Can Be" slogan to "An Army of One," in an effort to identify with Millennials' individualism (Mui 2001).

Millennials place a higher value on the balance between work and professional life than previous generations. To attract employees, companies are providing unique benefits such as flexible work arrangements and fitness allowances (Rushowy 2007). Lengthy vacation time is another example of benefits Millennials desire (Shellenbarger 2007). To satisfy the changing expectations of the new generation, employers have added incentives to job packages including extra vacation and flex scheduling (Gerdes 2007a). Moreover, companies and employees are capitalizing on new work structures made possible by advancements in technology (Gale 2007).

In order to boost their appeal, employers are altering benefits packages offered. For example, Lockheed Martin nearly tripled its applicant pool by increasing vacation time and improving an existing mentorship program in 2005. Similarly, Lockheed Martin and other companies now provide an option for flexible scheduling in order to satisfy the desired requirements of the new generation (Gerdes 2006).

To gain the most desirable graduates, companies not only elevate salary and benefits, they also highlight their corporate culture as well as the company's commitment to social responsibility, diversity, and environmental awareness. Companies may display their altruistic endeavors as a means to attract Millennials.

Millennials define a successful work life as one with three to five different careers (Gale 2007). Furthermore, job descriptions should list skills that will be learned, not the career path itself (Hulett 2006). Transferable or mobile skills are more attractive. The best companies offer the opportunity to transfer laterally within the company, allowing employees to build their skill sets. Millennials are more likely to experiment with different career paths and may apply for positions in various industries. As a result, Millennials may require employers to compete for them outside of industry boundaries (Gerdes 2006).

Employers unable to meet recruiting or retention goals will need to adapt to the changing expectations of the new generation. At NY Life Insurance, only 3 percent of interns accepted full-time positions in 2006. Unlike the previously pampered class of recruits, current interns will be required to take business etiquette classes and work longer hours, giving them a more realistic experience of the workplace (Gerdes 2007a). Additionally, companies will need to increase vacation and job flexibility in order to attract the best of the available Millennials. For example, Merck continued to offer ten vacation days when competitors offered 15, which resulted in challenges for Merck's recruiters (Gerdes 2006). With training costs averaging $10,000 per new hire, companies cannot afford to lose candidates to other companies because of better benefits packages.

Millennials entering the workforce, expect companies to "make the job fun" (Hulett 2006). Adding fitness centers or cafes may make the office more inviting, which may also make long hours seem less intimidating (Shellenbarger 2007). The concept of fun in the workplace can also extend to company-sponsored hobbies, sports teams, and volunteer opportunities (Hulett 2006). Increasingly, companies are allowing a designated amount of volunteer time to be performed while on the corporate clock. For example, Wells Fargo employees can volunteer at local schools during the regular workday without pay reductions (Gerdes 2006). Companies that allow employees to enhance workforce skills by applying those skills to service projects should highlight these opportunities during recruiting (Trunk 2007). For other companies, encouraging an entrepreneurial attitude will provide an atmosphere of creative freedom, something that made 3M Corporation famous years ago. Currently, Google, Inc. has continued the tradition by allowing all employees to take one day per week to develop or work on their own idea (Gerdes 2006).

As Millennials begin to fill the void of retiring generations, the age at which employees reach a supervisor level is decreasing. Because of the decreasing age of managerial-level employees, young supervisors may face situations in which they do not have experience. A lack of understanding about the legality of their actions in terms of hiring and terminating functions may prove challenging for them, which may also put companies at risk. To ensure legal understanding and prevent chaos, it is important to provide appropriate training to ensure employees have the skills necessary to succeed as managers (Lies 2007).

While recruiting is a challenge, retaining employees is an even greater one. More than one-third of new hires leave within three years. To overcome retention problems, unique offers such as compensation time and flexible work schedules must be developed. While Millennials are not generally perceived as being loyal, research has shown that such behavior can be developed through increased feedback and recognition (Hulett 2006). Belle Rose Ragins, a Professor of Human Resource Management at the University of Wisconsin-Milwaukee says, "[The] Millennials' psychological contract is with the relationships embedded within the organization, not the organization itself" (Berfield 2007).

Interviews with young employees have shown that job-hopping primarily occurs when they feel they have no options and must find better opportunities elsewhere (Trunk 2007). This is often influenced by boredom or disrespect (Gale 2007). Employees will rarely try to change things, so the burden remains upon employers to set up a system that promotes success. This system results in better employee retention. Employers should organize Millennials into a group or team environment and provide structured work with feedback (Jayson 2006). Career mentoring and assistance is a small price to pay when considering the costs associated with hiring and training a new employee. Additionally, in order to make internal promotions available and, therefore, possibly increase retention levels, companies such as Deloitte now offer programs to help employees find their path (Trunk 2007).

In the uncertain economic climate of today's business world, it can be difficult to retain employees who are significant contributors but are also susceptible to high levels of stress and/or depression (Twenge & Campbell 2008). Even if companies are able to keep such employees, their productivity levels are not ideal (Twenge & Campbell 2008). There are ways that businesses can combat the detrimental effects of stress and depression in the workplace. Examples of such programs include providing health benefits that cover emotional issues, specifically work- and home-related stress. Wang et al. conducted a study in 2007on a group of depressed employees. The study revealed that the employees were more likely to refrain from taking extra leave if their employer provided some sort of active intervention program, namely programs that provided employees with assistance to help them manager stressors in a healthy way (Twenge & Campbell 2008).

As previous chapters have addressed, the need for meeting each generation's specific values and expectations is key to the success of any company. Without addressing each of their outlined desires, companies will be unable to recruit the best and the brightest members of younger generations and will also find it difficult to retain those they already employ. For example, it has been found that "the younger [generational cohorts] may tend to seek out work opportunities that supply freedom and autonomy and may be prepared to leave the organisation (sic) if these needs are not met" (Cennamo & Gardner 2008). This clearly illustrates the willingness of the Millennial generation to leave a job if they feel their needs are not fully met.

It is vital to satisfy each generation's expectations; however, specific focus should be placed upon designing benefits and job structures that reflect the expectations and values of younger generations as they are the future of the workforce. Creating an organizational culture conducive to meeting both personal and organizational values enables companies to increase the perceived fit of a job by their employees. For example, it has been found that "a lack of person–organization (P-O) values fit may lead to reduced job satisfaction and commitment [in addition to] increas[ing the intention to leave]" (Cennamo & Gardner 2008). Due to the lack of focus in this key area, companies are putting themselves at risk of losing their younger employees (Cennamo & Gardner 2008). Failing to address person–organization fit further permeates the stereotypic depiction of the young generations' lack of commitment to any given organization.

As Millennials continue to confirm their desire to fully develop personal education and skill sets, the opportunity to learn within an organization is becoming increasingly appealing and important. While this holds true, MIllenials are not the only generation that appreciates the opportunity to further their education. While generational trends lend themselves to the substantiation of this fact, the aspiration to learn can also vary on an individual basis. Studies show that "learning in organizations is related to organizational commitment and intention to remain with the organization" (D'Amato & Herzfeldt 2008). Providing employees with the opportunity to better themselves through training, mentoring programs, and education may initially impose costs on the business, but in the long run will prevent the expense of losing employees and the related cost of retraining new hires.

It is a well-known fact that in order to recruit the best employees, companies must offer a competitive compensation package that addresses both intrinsic and extrinsic values. D'Amato & Herzfeldt state that extrinsic values like monetary compensations and benefits, promotions, and the provision of a company cell phone or car can greatly contribute to the attractiveness of an organization when recruiting new employees (2008). In terms of intrinsic values, they found the provision of "increased flexibility in work-at-home options, [giving employees] control over their schedules, and additional opportunities to develop skills and knowledge during work time or through employer-funded educational programs" also increases the attractiveness of a company during the recruitment process (D'Amato & Herzfeldt 2008).

Managers who have a strong grasp on the importance of instilling a strong sense of organizational commitment in their employees will experience much greater success in terms of recruitment and retention. Additionally, managers must build an environment conducive to an independent work structure that enables employees to make choices and allows them to meet their personal needs, contribute to the company as a whole, and show their organizational commitment.

Robert Half International conducted a study that enabled it to provide specific strategies and tactics to be used when recruiting and retaining members of the Millennial generation. The first strategy is to "make them an offer they can't refuse" ("Generation Y" 2008). Essentially, this means that companies must provide job offers that address the main career concerns of this generational cohort. This study identified the top career concerns as financial security, job stability, and career satisfaction listed as most important to least important ("Generation Y" 2008).

The next tip provided is to "put yourself in their shoes when thinking about benefits" ("Generation Y" 2008). This indicates that managers will be more successful if they provide benefits that the Millennial generation deems important. These benefits include "healthcare coverage, paid vacation, dental care coverage, 401(k) programs, bonuses, and flexible work hours/telecommuting" ("Generation Y" 2008).

The third tactic is to "show them how they can grow." As each chapter thus far has reinforced, the importance of providing an environment and job structure in which Millennials can fully expand their skills is vitally important. This environment includes aspects such as mentoring programs, challenging and diverse work assignments, and the cultivation of reciprocal work relationships ("Generation Y" 2008).

Finally, Robert Half International recommends that companies "get the word out" ("Generation Y" 2008). Because of the vast use of technology by younger generations, companies can no longer rely on the traditional recruiting tactics that once served them well. Instead, focus should be placed on cutting-edge recruitment through the utilization of the Internet, blogs, social networking, podcasts, and so on. When recruiting, companies need to advertise their corporate image, providing a clear idea of what Millennials can expect to experience if they work for the company ("Generation Y" 2008). By reaching out to talented Millennials through such channels, companies are more likely to attain the employees that will be successful once hired.

While it is a well-accepted fact that Millennials have expectations of being mentored within the workplace, they also want to share their skills and talents with others in the company. Companies that have implemented reverse mentorship programs, allowing younger generations to share their knowledge with older and more established employees, have experienced great success. These programs enabled older employees to learn "technical skills" (such as Internet and email skills), but even more importantly "learned valuable insights into how both younger staffers and the marketplace perceived the firm" (Patota, Schwartz, & Schwartz 2007). As companies that have already implemented such programs have shown, these types of programs can be extremely helpful in retaining young employees. "These types of programs have shown the value of treating generational differences as a competitive advantage to enhance creativity rather than as a source of conflict and misunderstanding" (Patota, Schwartz, & Schwartz 2007).

In this day and age, managers face the challenge of simultaneously motivating several generations at the same time. This can present a variety of difficulties; however, "with an appropriate mindset, the potential areas of conflict [can] be viewed as a source of a rich and rewarding work environment" (Patota, Schwartz, & Schwartz 2007).

Due to different expectations and concepts of success in the workplace, motivational tactics differ between generations. The differences in personality each generation exhibits may determine motivational factors; however, many of the observed discrepancies can be attributed to the life stage of each generation rather than the generational group itself (Wong et al. 2008). It has been shown that work values change as generations mature and cycle through different phases of their lives.

Proof of this can be seen through the cyclical nature of the way each generation is viewed as it enters the workforce. Currently, it is a common belief that Millennials require more attention than past generations. However, before the Millennial generation joined the workforce, Generation X was perceived as "demanding" too for several reasons. First, in terms of the speed at which they expected the organization to operate, their perception contrasted older generations' viewpoints because of their focus on the technological advances with which they grew up. Secondly, Generation X felt that career progression should be based on capability rather than tenure, so they expected to climb the corporate ladder at a faster pace.

Since the Millennials have become the newest addition to corporate America, Generation X now appears to be patient and less demanding. Millennials are perceived as having a general attitude that results should be instantaneous and deliverables should be provided immediately. The immense reliance on technology that this group of young people has been accustomed to throughout their lives contributes heavily to their expectation of immediate results.

Due to the length of time the Traditionalist generation has been in the workforce, they prefer to be recognized based on their expertise and viewed as valued employees within the organization (Dittman 2005). Baby Boomers want to know that they are valued and important to the success of the company. This can be accomplished though recognition of their dedication, demonstrated through their long hours and corporate know-how (Hymowitz 2007). On the other hand, Generation X likes to explore out-of-the-box solutions and to be recognized for their originality or technological expertise.

Millennials like to collaborate and want praise for their teamwork, creativity, and commitment (Dittmann 2005). They have been raised in an environment in which they expect praise "because they're used to it—and crave it"

(Rushowy 2007). Managers complain that new Millennial hires want promotions, larger salaries, and fast-paced careers soon after they are hired. Millennials have a different concept of what paying dues means and how that plays into climbing the corporate ladder.

Environments that promote creativity and independent thinking are appealing to the Millennials cohort (Armour 2005). They have a "strong work ethic" when they feel supported by their supervisors and co-workers (Hulett 2006). Programs that provide new employees the opportunity to take control of their career and envision a future, satisfies this generational cohort's desires. In addition to creating motivation, employees may find such programs open lines of communication with supervisors regarding goals and future advancement.

8 Managerial Styles

In the workplace, when differences of opinion arise, they are regularly attributed to gender, age, race, religion, personality, or leadership style, but rarely is generational difference taken into account (Lancaster & Stillman 2002). However, when it is considered that over 60 percent of employers have cited tension between employees because of generational diversity, this is clearly a pertinent problem (Armour 2005). Intergenerational conflict is troubling in the workplace because it may keep plans, projects, or ideas from being implemented or from progressing (Dittmann 2005). It can also lead to increased turnover rates, problems with hiring, communication difficulty, and poor morale (Lancaster & Stillman 2002). Many offices require team environments, which can provide a breeding ground for intergenerational problems. Ultimately, working with multiple generations in the workplace requires managerial awareness to develop diverse expectations and styles.

Intergenerational workforces require managers to use multiple management styles because each generation, like each person, is unique (Hymowitz 2007). Managers should keep in mind that age is not the only factor that differentiates employees from one another. An employee's success depends upon the efforts put forth by their managers to know each individual well enough to understand their strengths, weaknesses, and needs on the job (Hulett 2006).

Every manager must use proper performance-appraisal techniques in order to monitor and track the progress and productivity of each employee. Although many evaluation techniques have been widely accepted in the past, no single method is necessarily 100 percent accurate. As Millennials have joined the workforce, managers are now facing an additional challenge. Although self-evaluations became popular in recent years, this type of evaluation is predicted to be unsuccessful with this new generation. This is a direct result of the way Millennials view themselves and, specifically, their talents and skills. Instead, "360 degree feedback (from managers, co-workers, direct reports, and customers) has become the standard with the most effective 360 degree feedback tools based on behaviors that other employees can see" (Twenge & Campbell 2008).

Throughout the past few decades, corporate corruption has become more and more apparent to the public and employees. Corporations no longer have the squeaky clean image they once possessed. Instead, they may be perceived as being capable of great wrongdoing simply based on the fact that the once trusted images of corporate America have been lost. In order for managers to combat this negative image internally and gain the trust and loyalty of their employees, they "need to make ethics an explicit part of their leadership program by visibly and intentionally role modeling ethical behavior, and holding followers accountable for ethical conduct" (Twenge & Campbell 2008).

As was explained in Chapter 4, the expectations and values of each generation can vary greatly. Today's managers are forced to find a way in which they can effectively connect with employees from each generational cohort and connect the members of those cohorts with one another. It is vital that they identify and use managerial techniques that are appropriate to the expectations and values of each generation. Some methods currently being practiced include coaching, mentoring, frequent evaluation, and feedback, and the use of public employee recognition (Twenge & Campbell 2008).

Although the hands-on methods of management appear to be more effective in reaching each generation, specifically Millennials, managers face the risk of creating the problem of "rust out" (Twenge & Campbell 2008). "Rust out—in some ways the opposite of burnout—creates employees who are not motivated or satisfied and ultimately results in poor performance for the organization" (Twenge & Campbell 2008). In addition to the risk of providing too much feedback, managers may also create this problem by failing to assign their employees challenging tasks and allowing them to function autonomously. The key is for managers to find the delicate balance between providing a sufficient amount of support while still challenging their employees to push their boundaries and grow (Twenge & Campbell 2008).

It is common that older generations view Millennials as lacking work ethic or being uncommitted because they tend to work only the hours required of them (Dittmann 2005). This contrasts with the behavior of generations past that placed greater value on their work-life and sometimes neglected their personal obligations. As Baby Boomers retire, a loss of institutional knowledge and familiarity of the company can occur and may even leave a void that hurts the institution (Lies 2007). However, older generations must understand that conditions are different than previously existed. Managers who are now responsible for Millennial employees must throw away the preconceived notions of the past, and focus on the different way in which this new generational cohort needs to be managed.

Satisfying the expectations of Millennials requires that managers "[give] up control, [put] themselves in uncomfortable positions, and in general, [spend] an awful lot of time thinking about how to please," in addition to learning the best managerial techniques to utilize with the newest generation" (Gerdes 2007a). Many managers feel that the Millennial generation "expects office cultures to adapt to them," including managerial styles (Mui 2001). At the same time, great resentment commonly exists between 30-something managers and Millennials. This resentment is derived from the recessions that existed when many Generation X members came of age and the associated difficulty they had in finding work. They believe Millennials have "often had it easy, and it shows." Despite their complaints, the pay-your-dues mentality will not effectively integrate Millennials into the workplace. They prefer to know immediately what their direct contribution will be (Hulett 2006). As a result, they have been called the "Ritalin generation," where posting "speed limits in hallways" may be necessary, or accruing leave "in nanoseconds" must occur (Mui 2001).

Contrary to those beliefs, employers say that efficiency and positive job performance are important to Millennials (Gerdes 2006). For employees to be successful, it is important for managers to adapt their managerial styles to match each generational cohort's values. Due to the lofty goals they set and the technological era in which they have grown up, Millennials must be managed differently. Coaching and mentoring with plenty of positive feedback will be the most beneficial way for managers to reach this young generation (Rushowy 2007). This generation has a strict set of priorities. "They want to work, but they don't want work to be their life" (Armour 2005). By providing a flexible atmosphere with choices in terms of scheduling, duties, and priorities, managers may allow employees to feel they are contributing to the overall purpose of the organization and are in control of their futures (Hulett 2006).

Young employees also do not fear changes in the workplace, which allows for technological advancement. At the same time, when it comes to technology, Millennials must remember to "understand the perspectives of their managers" (Gale 2007). While Baby Boomers expect in-person or over-the-phone meetings, younger employees consider virtual options to be preferable (Armour 2005). While new ways of interacting with one another are made possible by advancing technology, Millennials do not recognize that these techno-centric communication methods are not necessarily the most effective ones.

However, there are two sides to this coin. Traditionalists and Baby Boomers are often perceived as being unwilling to utilize options made available through new technology. As a result, they are often times viewed as old fashioned and behind the times. "You have to position yourself not to say outdated things," says Lynne Lancaster, a consultant on generational issues and co-author of *When Generations Collide* (2002). When managers portray themselves as inflexible to change, they may lose respect of both younger employees and colleagues.

Despite being fresh out of college, Millennials are comfortable sharing opinions and providing major input when management is receptive to their feedback and viewpoints. Additionally, they do not like ambiguity or risk when assigned a project or task. They want to know specifics about job advancement, which can pose a challenge to managers to provide enough detail to satisfy this generational cohort. However, any honest conversation about workplace expectations is appreciated (Gerdes 2007a). New hires expect managers to be knowledgeable, listen to new ideas, inspire others, and recognize achievements of teams (Tulgan & Martin 2001). The more new employees learn and experience, the greater value they provide to the company. By explaining why they are performing certain tasks, managers can make Millennials feel more incorporated into projects and company goals (Gale 2007).

Inclusion is always a beneficial way to educate and train young employees. However, Millennials have a hard time distinguishing the line between boss and friend (Gerdes 2006). Due to being raised with "coddling and permissiveness," they view supervisors with less authority. Instead, authoritative individuals are seen more as friends or mentors. The best advice when working with Millennials is to try a coaching management style that includes small goals and deadlines, and increasing feedback and responsibility each time (Mui 2001). Additionally, specific boundaries should be set to define roles when necessary.

Millennials have been told that they can achieve anything, which has created a problem because they feel there are too many options available to them. Managers need to be aware of this and take it into consideration when determining the management style to use with this young generational cohort.

By allowing them pathways towards developing many of their skills and competencies, Millennials may be more interested in staying with a company for an extended period of time (Twenge & Campbell 2008).

Overall, there are several approaches managers can take when leading members of each generation. Traditionalists and Baby Boomers both thrive and respond well when the traditional managerial techniques are utilized. These groups both have appreciation for traditional hierarchies and authoritative leadership styles (Crampton & Hodge 2007).

Crampton and Hodge have provided a compilation of suggestions from various sources that focus specifically on Generation X and the Millennials. They provide information about the areas that fellow managers feel can be problematic, the techniques that are ineffective, and strategies that are best implemented for each cohort. Table 8.1 overleaf illustrates these suggestions in detail.

Each generation has different beliefs, expectations, values, learning styles, and desires. Managing employees that are members of several generations is not an easy task. However, it is the reality of the business world today. The creation of a culture and coordinating programs that foster communication and collaboration between all of the generations present in the workforce will help to alleviate the difficulties managers may encounter. The key to building a successful work place centers around building an environment in which employees can openly communicate with each and with management. In order to truly create a cohesive workplace managers must encourage employees to view generational difference as valuable strengths rather than weaknesses.

Table 8.1   Techniques and complaints about Generation X and Millennials

	Manager Complaints About Them	Ineffective Techniques	Suggested Strategies
Generation X	They ask why. They are unwilling to "pay their dues." They are unwilling to "go the extra mile." They are cynical and have a "dim" view of the world. They are not committed. They do not respect authority. They are far more interested in things other than their jobs. They want things now.	Fea-based management. Poor time management. Micro-management. Politically-based culture. Indirect communication. Opinions and ideas ignored. Prevalence of lip service, not action. Failure to give feedback and regular performance reviews. Meaningless raises. Insincere, gratuitous "thank-yous." People thrown into jobs without training. Not telling the "why's." "Because I said so" or similar attitudes.	Team-based management. Diversity. Exploration. Experimentation. The idea is the power, not the person. Team and individual credit. "Resume building" opportunities. Use email as a primary communication tool. Talk in short sound bites to keep their attention. Ask them for their feedback and provide them with regular feedback. Share information with them on a regular basis and keep them in the communication loop. Use an informal communication style that emphasizes the positive.

Table 8.1 **Techniques and complaints about Generation X and Millennials** *concluded*

	Manager Complaints About Them	Ineffective Techniques	Suggested Strategies
Millennials	Similar to Generation X. Sense of entitlement.	Not yet applicable.	Use action words to challenge them at every opportunity. Communicate using their preferred method—email. Seek their feedback constantly and provide them with regular feedback. Use humor and create a fun work environment. Encourage them to take risks and break the rules so that they can explore new ways of doing things. Let them know that what they do matters. Tell them the truth—don't try to pull the wool over their eyes. In order to get "buy in," explain the why of what you asking them to do and tell them what is in it for them. Learn their language; communicate in terms that they understand. Be on the lookout for "rewarding opportunities." Praise them in public—make them a "star." Make the workplace fun. Model behavior—don't expect one thing out of them that you don't and won't deliver yourself; be the example. Establish comfortable work environments, flexible work hours and project-centered rather than function-based responsibilities. Be flexible, challenging, creative, and empowering in your management style. Initiate programs geared toward reducing stress-related problems. Consider offering a cafeteria-style benefit package that allows for flexibility.

References

Anderson, N. & Schalk, R. (1998). The psychological contract in retrospect and prospect. *Journal of Organizational Behavior*, 19(S1), 637–647.

Argyris, C. (1960). *Understanding Organizational Behavior*. Homewood, IL: Dorsey.

Armour, S. (2005, November 6). Generation Y: They've arrived at work with a new attitude. *USA Today*. Retrieved October 23, 2007, from http://www.usatoday.com/money/workplace/2005-11-06-gen-y_x.htm.

Aschoff, S. (2006, May 26). Greater than 'The Greatest'? *St. Petersburg Times*. St. Petersburg, FL: Times Publishing Company. Retrieved August 28, 2007 from *Lexis Nexis*.

Berfield, S. (2007, September 9). How one company bridges the generation gap. *Business Week* [online]. Los Angeles: McGraw Hill Companies, Inc. Retrieved October 23, 2007 from http://www.businessweek.com/careers/content/sep2007/ca2007099_741888.htm.

Blain, A. (n.d.). The Millennial tidalwave: Five elements that will change the workplace tomorrow. *Journal of the Quality Assurance Institute*. 11–13.

Blancero, D. M. & Johnson, S. A. (2001). A process model of discretionary service behavior integrating psychological contracts, organizational justice, and customer feedback to manage service agents. *Journal of Quality Management*, 6(2), 307–329.

Bounds, W. (2000, August 9). Buying Gen Y: Rushing to cash in on the new baby boom—a bumper crop of U.S. kids boast more marketing clout than their Boomer parents. *The Wall Street Journal*. Retrieved October 23, 2007 from *ProQuest*.

Braid, M. (2007, May 20). How to connect with Generation Y. *Times Online*. Retrieved October 25, 2007 from http://www.timesonline.co.uk/tol/life_and_style/career_and_jobs/recruiter_forum/article1813031.ece.

Cavanaugh, M. A. & Noe, R. A. (1999). Antecedents and consequences of the new psychological contract. *Journal of Organizational Behavior*, 20(3), 323–340.

Cennamo, L. & Gardner, D. (2008). Generational differences in work values, outcomes and person-organisation values fit. *Journal of Managerial Psychology*, 23(8), 891–906.

Chen, K. (2001, June 12). A special news report about life on the job—and trends taking shape there. *The Wall Street Journal*. New York: Dow Jones & Company, Inc. Retrieved October 23, 2007 from *ProQuest*.

Chrobot-Mason, D. & Leslie, J. B. (2003). The role of multicultural competence and emotional intelligence in managing diversity. Presented at the 2003 meeting of the Society for Industrial and Organizational Psychology, Orlando, FL.

Coyle-Shapiro, J. & Kessler, I. (2000). Consequences of the psychological contract for the employment relationship: A large-scale survey. *Journal of Management Studies*, 37(7), 903–930.

Crampton, S. M. & Hodge, J. W. (2007). Generations in the workplace: Understanding age diversity. *The Business Review*, 9(1), 16–22.

D'Amato, A. & Herzfeldt, R. (2008). Learning orientation, organizational commitment and talent retention across. *Journal of Managerial Psychology*, 23(8), 929–953.

Dencker, J. C., Joshi, A. & Martocchio, J. J. (2007). Employee benefits as context for intergenerational conflict. *Human Resource Management Review*, 17, 208–220.

Dencker, J. C., Joshi, A. & Martocchio, J. J. (2008). Towards a theoretical framework linking generational memories to workplace attitudes and behaviors. *Human Resource Management Review*, 18(3), 180–187.

Dittmann, M. (2005, June 6). Generational Differences at Work. *Monitor on Psychology*, 36(7), 54. Retrieved August 28, 2007 from http://apa.org/monitor/jun05/generational.html.

Dries, N., Pepermans, R., & De Kerpel, E. (2008). Exploring four generations' beliefs about career: Is "satisfied" the new "successful"? *Journal of Managerial Psychology*, 23(8), 907–928.

Frazier, M. (2007, February 5). Locked in a cultural battle of the ages. *Advertising Age, 78*(6), 29. Retrieved August 28, 2007 from *Ebsco Host*.

Gale, S. F. (2007, March). Bridging the gap. *PM Network*, 21(3), 26–31. Retrieved August 28, 2007 from *Ebsco Host*.

"Gen Yers changing the face of the workplace". (2007, September 9). *The Sunday Journal*. Albuquerque, NM: Journal Publishing Co.

"Generation Gap in the Workplace." (2007, July). *Promo, 20(7)*, 66. Retrieved August 28, 2007 from *Ebsco Host*.

"Generation Y what millennial workers want: How to attract and retain Gen Y employees." (2008). Menlo Park, CA: Robert Half International.

Gerdes, L. (2006, September 18). The best places to launch a career. *Business Week*. 64–80. Los Angeles: McGraw Hill Companies, Inc. Retrieved August 28, 2007 from *Ebsco Host*.

Gerdes, L. (2007a, September 13). The best places to launch a career. *Business Week*. Special Report. Los Angeles: McGraw Hill Companies, Inc. Retrieved October 23, 2007 from http://www.businessweek.com/careers/content/sep2007/ca20070913_595536.htm?chan=careers_special+report+---+best+places+to+launch+a+ career_best+places+to+launch +a+career.

Gerdes, L. (2007b, September 13). The college administrator: What's different about the Ys. *Business Week*. Special Report. Los Angeles: McGraw Hill Companies, Inc. Retrieved October 23, 2007 from http://www.businessweek.com/careers/content/sep2007/ca20070913_426598.htm.

Greenberg, J. (2001). Studying organizational justice cross-culturally: Fundamental challenges. *International Journal of Conflict Management*, 12(4), 365–375.

Griffin, L. J. (2004). "Generations and Collective Memory" Revisited: Race, region, and memory of civil rights. *American Sociological Review*, 69(4), 544–557.

Guest, D. E. (1998). Is the psychological contract worth taking seriously? *Journal of Organizational Behavior*, 19(S1), 649–664.

Herriot, P. & Pemberton, C. (1995). *New Deals: The revolution in managerial careers*, Chichester: Wiley

Howe, N. & Strauss, W. (2007). The next 20 years: How customer and workforce attitudes will evolve. *Harvard Business Review*, 41–52.

Hulett, K. J. (2006, November). They are here to replace us: Recruiting and retaining Millennials. *Journal of Financial Planning, 17*. Retrieved August 28, 2007 from *Ebsco Host*.

Hymowitz, C. (2007, July 9). Managers find ways to get generations to close culture gaps. *The Wall Street Journal*. Retrieved October 23, 2007 from *ProQuest*.

Jayson, S. (2006, June 29). The 'Millennials' come of age; Experts: Generation shows great potential. *USA Today*. Retrieved August 28, 2007 from *Lexis Nexis*.

Kertzer, D. I. (1983). Generation as a sociological problem. *Annual Review of Sociology, 9*, 125–149.

Lancaster, L. C., & Stillman, D. (2002). *When Generations Collide*. New York: HarperBusiness.

Lane, A. (2006, June 5). Business Looks to Adapt to Needs of New Generation. *Crain's Detroit Business*. Detroit: Crain Communications. Retrieved August 28, 2007 from *Lexis Nexis*.

Lester, S. W., Turnley, W. H. & Bloodgood, J. M. (2002). Not seeing eye to eye: Differences in supervisor and subordinate perceptions of and attributions for psychological contract breach. *Journal of Organizational Behavior*, 23(1), 39–56.

Levinson, H., Price, C. R., Munden, K. J. & Stolley, C. M. (1962). *Men, Management and Mental Health*. Cambridge, MA: Harvard University Press.

Lewis-McClear, K. & Taylor, M. S. (1997). Not seeing eye-to-eye: Implications of discrepant psychological contracts and contract violation for the employment relationship. Proceedings of the Academy of Management meetings, Vancouver.

Lies, II, M. A. (2007, September). Bye bye Baby Boomers! Replacing supervisor skills. *Employee Benefit Plan Review*, 5–6. New York: Aspen Publishers Inc. Retrieved October 23, 2007 from *Ebsco Host*.

Masterson, S. S. (2001). A trickle-down model of organizational justice: Relating employees' and customers perceptions of reactions to fairness. *Journal of Applied Psychology*, 86(4), 594–604.

Morrison, E. W. & Robinson, S. L. (1997). When employees feel betrayed: A model of how psychological contract violation develops. *Academy of Management Review*, 22(1), 226–256.

Mui, N. (2001, February 4). Here come the kids: Gen Y invades the workplace. *The New York Times*. Retrieved October 23, 2007 from *ProQuest*.

Mueller, S. L. & Clarke, L.D. (1998). Political-economic context and sensitivity to equity: Differences between the United States and the transition economies of central and eastern Europe. *Academy of Management Journal*, 41, 319–329.

Patota, N., Schwartz, D. & Schwartz, T. (2007). Leveraging generational differences for productivity gains. *Journal of American Academy of Business*, 11(2), 1–10.

Portwood, J. D. & Miller, E. L. (1979). Evaluating the psychological contract: Its implications for employee satisfaction and work behavior. Proceedings of the Academy of Management meetings.

Robinson, S. L., Kraatz, M. S. & Rousseau, D. M. (1994). Changing obligations and the psychological contract: A longitudinal study. *Academy of Management Journal*, 37(1), 137–152.

Robinson, S. L. & Morrison, E. W. (2000). The development of psychological contract breach violation: A longitudinal study. *Journal of Organizational Behavior*, 21(5), 525–546.

Robinson, S. L. & Rousseau, D. M. (1994). Violating the psychological contract: not the exception but the norm. *Journal of Organizational Behavior*, 15(3), 245–259.

Rousseau, D. M. (1990). New hire perceptions of their own and their employer's obligations: a study of psychological contracts. *Journal of Organizational Behavior*, 11(5), 389–400.

Rousseau, D. M. (1995). *Psychological Contracts in Organizations: Understanding Written and Unwritten Agreements.* Newbury Park, CA: Sage.

Rousseau, D. M. (1998). The 'problem' of the psychological contract considered. *Journal of Organizational Behavior,* 19(S1), 665–671.

Rousseau, D. M. (2001). The Idiosyncratic deal: Flexibility versus fairness? *Organizational Dynamics*, 29(4), 260–273.

Rousseau, D. M. & Anton, R. J. (1988). Fairness and implied contract obligations in job terminations: A policy-capturing study. *Human Performance*, 1(4), 273–289.

Rousseau, D. M. & Anton, R. J. (1991). Fairness and implied contract obligations in job terminations: The role of contributions, promises, and performance. *Journal of Organizational Behavior*, 12(4), 287–299.

Rousseau, D. M. & McLean Parks, J. (1993). The contract of individuals and organizations. In L. L. Cummings & B. M. Staw (ed.) *Research in Organizational Behavior*, 15, 1–43.

Rousseau, D. M. & Schalk R. eds. (2001). *Psychological Contracts in Employment: Cross-National Perspectives.* Thousand Oaks, CA: Sage.

Rousseau, D. M. & Tijoriwala, S. A. (1996). Assessing psychological contracts: Issues, alternatives and measures. *Journal of Organizational Behavior*, 19(S1), 679–695.

Rushowy, K. (2007, June 9). At work, it's all about positive feedback; Old ways of doing business won't attract or keep Millennials, who crave praise from their employers. *Toronto Star.* Retrieved August 28, 2007 from *Lexis Nexis.*

Sanchez, J. I. & Brock, P. (1996). Outcomes of perceived discrimination among Hispanic employees: Is diversity management a luxury or a necessity? *Academy of Management Journal*, 39(3), 704–720.

Schein, E. H. (1965, 1990). *Organizational Psychology*. Englewood Cliffs, NJ: Prentice-Hall.

Schuman, H. & Scott, J. (1989). Generations and collective memories. *American Sociological Review,* 54(3), 359–381.

Schuman, H. & Scott, J. (2004). Cohorts, chronology, and collective memories. *Public Opinion Quarterly,* 68(2), 217–254.

Shellenbarger, S. (2007, October 4). What makes a company a great place to work today. *The Wall Street Journal.* New York: Dow Jones & Company, Inc. Retrieved October 23, 2007 from *ProQuest*.

Swann, D. T. (2007, April 23). Generation Me does plenty for others. *The Boston Globe*. Boston: Globe Newspaper Company. Retrieved August 28, 2007 from *Lexis Nexis*.

Thomas, D. C. & Au, K. (2000). Cultural variation in the psychological contract. Proceedings of the Academy of Management meetings, Washington, D.C.

Trunk, P. (2007, July 5). What Gen Y really wants. *Time*. Retrieved October 23, 2007 from http://www.time.com/time/magazine/article/0,9171,1640395,00.html.

Tulgan, B. & Martin, C. A. (2001). *Managing Generation Y: Global Citizens Born in the Late Seventies and Early Eighties*. Amherst, MA: Human Resources Development Press.

Turnley, W. H. & Feldman, D. C. (1999). The impact of contract violations on exit, voice, loyalty, and neglect. *Human Relations*, 52(7), 895–922.

Turnley, W. H. & Feldman, D. C. (2000). Re-examining the effects of psychological contract violations: Unmet expectations and job dissatisfaction. *Journal of Organizational Behavior*, 21(1), 25–42.

Twenge, J. M. & Campbell, S. M. (2008). Generational differences in psychological traits and their impact on the workplace. *Journal of Managerial Psychology*, 23(8), 862–877.

Underwood, C. (2007, July). Bridging the generation gaps. *American Gas*, 89(6), 42–43. Retrieved August 28, 2007 from *Ebsco Host*.

Wang, P. S., Simon, G. E., Avorn, J., Azocar, F., Ludman, E. J., McCulloch, J., Petukhova, M. Z., & Keller, R. C. (2007). Telephone screening, outreach, and care management for depressed workers and impact on clinical and work productivity outcomes. *Journal of the American Medical Association*, 298, 1401–1411.

Westerman, J. W., and Yamamura, J. H. (2007). Generational preferences for work environment fit: effects on employee outcomes. *Career Development International*, 12(2), 150–161.

"What Generation Gap? Many Workers Don't See One." (2006, December). *HR Focus, 83(12)*, 9. Retrieved August 28, 2007 from *Ebsco Host*.

Wolfe Morrison, E. & Robinson, S. L. (1997). When employees feel betrayed: A model of how psychological contract violation develops. *Academy of Management Review*, 22(1), 226–256.

Wong, M., Gardiner, E., Lang, W. and Coulon, L. (2008). Generational differences in personality and motivation: Do they exist and what are the implications for the workplace? *Journal of Managerial Psychology,* 23(8), 878–890.

Index